The

MEASURE

of my

POWERS

The

MEASURE

of my

POWERS

A MEMOIR
OF FOOD, MISERY,
AND PARIS

JACKIE KAI ELLIS

appetite
by RANDOM HOUSE

Appetite by Random House® and colophon are registered trademarks of Penguin Random House LLC.

Library and Archives of Canada Cataloguing in Publication is available upon request.
ISBN: 978-0-147-53039-4
eBook ISBN: 978-0-147-53040-0

Cover and book design: Lisa Jager
Cover and book photography: Jackie Kai Ellis
Printed and bound in Canada

Published in Canada by Appetite by Random House®,
a division of Penguin Random House Canada Limited.

www.penguinrandomhouse.ca

10 9 8 7 6 5 4

I dedicate this book to two people:

1. To M. F. K. Fisher, whose stories validated the beauty in living, inspiring me to do so.

2. To you, who may find yourself in this story. Inspiring you to find beauty in your own life would bring so much more to mine.

CONTENTS

PREFACE

When I was first asked to write a memoir, I declined immediately. I was scared. Though, I was not afraid to recount my experiences in a Parisian pastry school, or of the opening of Beaucoup Bakery & Café, The Paris Tours, or even of how I became a writer. Over coffee, interviews, speeches, and articles, I shared these stories proudly.

I could easily tell the happier, abbreviated versions of my memories, the ones with easy endings, because I assumed no one would be interested in the others. I was concerned about making others feel awkward if I was more candid. These struggles were painful to live and I presumed they were just as uncomfortable to hear—sometimes seeing another's vulnerability accentuates our own. Truthfully, I was worried about what others might think of me. I wanted so desperately to be special, but I imagined they would see my flaws and weaknesses and think that I was unremarkable, and at the time, sometimes even now, a childish part of me was afraid of being judged.

So instead, I offered an excuse: my story is not yet done. But deep down inside, I knew I wanted to write it, and in reality our stories are rarely finished anyway.

I spent years skipping over the painful parts until I realized that, in those moments when I was telling my story, it was I who wasn't ready to remember these harder moments in such detail. I had carefully put those darker memories away in a sturdy box and placed it in the back of a closet. It was a way to protect myself from the immense hurt that, at one time, I was drowning in, day after day. And I tried to forget these stories existed, ignoring them for as long as I could, tiptoeing around them, careful not to kick up their terrible dust.

After a few years passed, some of the hurt had healed, and I felt strong enough to peek inside the box again. I looked at the painful parts and grew to appreciate that my strength was found in the moments when I felt weakest, and that they were both beautifully and crucially intertwined. I began to understand that by refusing to write this memoir, I was only trying to avoid vulnerability. That was, frankly, not a good enough reason for me. So, knowing I was braver than my fears, I began to write, and when I did, I naturally thought of M. F. K. Fisher.

As I reread her books, I found myself once again in the pains and joys of her narratives. I was drawn again into her stories of Sunday picnics by swimming holes, eating peach pie with her silent father; of prewar France, warming segments of clementine on radiators while watching soldiers soldier on the streets below her bedroom window. I found myself laughing, amused by her sharp sense of humor—she titled one of her chapters "Pity the Blind in Palate." I was taken by the way she placed modest words beside one another to create images, tastes, and smells so whole that I could have sworn the memories were my own.

When I first read her stories, those many years ago during the emptiest time in my life, Fisher's work led me, page by page, into her world, and the stories were my connection to the living.

They held onto me, like a thick rope tight around my wrist as I hovered in the depths of depression. They pulled me to food, into the kitchen to bake, cook, console, feed, feast, and connect back to who I was.

It was then, in that hungry and confused place, that I read this quote from George Santayana: "To be happy you must have taken the measure of your powers, tasted the fruits of your passion, and learned your place in the world." And when I began this book, less hungry, having tasted passions and discovered places in the world where I felt at home, I reread this same quote and knew these words were also mine.

M. F. K. Fisher's book *The Gastronomical Me* titles eleven of its twenty-six chapters "The Measure of My Powers," and I chose that as the title of my book, as an ode to her and how her words have fed me.

And like many of hers, my book is a collection of memories. I've written them as vignettes, short or long stories strung together with food. They are at times playful, at others painful, and like memories, they are sometimes seemingly unrelated and random. Though this is just the way we remember: while doing something mundane, like brushing our teeth or during our commute, non-sequential memories surface, at times taking us by surprise. But the memories we do keep form who we are when all put together like a puzzle, regardless of how unimportant and vague each one seems alone.

It was through writing that I was placed again in the depths of those moments I had tried so hard to forget. I found some parts flowed easily, but at other points I was obstinate, refusing to move until I gave myself the space to remember, to let go, to forgive others and myself before I could tell the story with any amount of clarity and grace. And with each chapter, I celebrated again my

triumphs, relived my passions, and said goodbye once more. Slowly, word by word, my story and I were made whole again. In the end, I found that writing this book was more helpful to me than it could ever be to anyone else.

Even so, I share my stories, as honestly as I remember them, in the hopes that someone might read it on a day when it might be particularly helpful. Or that perhaps those who recognize my darkest moments may also find themselves in my triumphs, and be fed until their hungers are satisfied.

JKE

A NOTE ON THE NAMES AND CONVERSATIONS IN THIS BOOK

I purposely chose not to share names, using only a single letter instead, for many people in this book, particularly for my former husband, G. The reason is that this story is mine and not theirs. The conversations and details are as accurate as I remember them, but as we all know, memories evolve and grow as we do, blue turns teal, and I know that for my entire future, I will only see richer facets of the past.

CHOCOLATE CHIP COOKIE

{2007}

THE JOURNEY OF A THOUSAND MILES

begins with a SINGLE STEP.

L a o - T z u

THESE WERE THE TWO MOMENTS IN MY DAY I DREADED—
no, I think "feared" is a better word—most: the moment just
before sleep and the precise moment I woke up. The unnerving
silence of those times. There were no busy sounds to distract me,
and nothing to occupy my mind. They were the moments I would
be forced to face my own tangled and disfigured mind, even
though I wanted desperately to look away.

At night I would lie awake sometimes until the dark sky
lightened into paler shades of dawn. My insides crawled and
vibrated, panic hijacking hours that, for others, were filled with
easy rest. Even when I did find sleep, usually on the couch with
the artificial noises of late-night TV lulling me, it was never for
very long.

In the morning my chest would clench and yearn for uncon-
sciousness. I kept my eyes closed and my body still, like a corpse,
in hopes that my fragile sleep wouldn't leave me completely. I tried
to remember the last lingering image, any residue of a dream,
wanting it to pull me back for another moment or two, but I was
always out of luck and would quickly realize the effort was in
vain. I hadn't dreamt in months. In the past, my dreams had been
wild and vivid: full of colors, conversations, places, the feel of
fabric between my fingertips, or even the faces of people I had

long forgotten. I would dream of a friend's hazel eyes speckled with rust, or of the fine hairs at the back of their neck that formed a V. But these dreams had stopped, and so had sleep, with restlessness replacing both almost entirely. I was abandoned and forced to be alive for another day, so I would relent and slowly open my eyes to my dark, damp bedroom.

Inhale. Exhale.

"I can do this. Just get through today . . . and then after today . . ." I paused to imagine what came next. There was only a repeating image of a lifeless routine that made me feel nauseated.

"Tomorrow it starts all over again." Dread filled me. I closed my eyes again, sinking into myself, wishing I could cry, but mostly, that ability had abandoned me too. "I have to do this over and over again, and again, and again," I thought to myself, G sprawled to my left, the sheets, humid from his sweat, covering me like thick, cold skin.

"When does this end?" Inhale. Exhale.

Light was so unbearable to G that he had dark blinds installed on every window in our two-bedroom apartment. Greater than his dislike for light, though, was his loathing of materialism and superfluous "things." So there was no artwork on the walls of our room, there weren't any family photos or night tables for them to sit on, only a bed and a generic Swedish floor lamp in the corner. And every single morning, I awoke in this beige room, with bare beige walls and carpets that were an ever-so-slightly lighter shade of beige. I opened my eyes to nothing but emptiness in an empty room, numb with only the feeling of moist blankets cradling me.

I pleaded silently to God, to anything that might help me. "All I need is one thing, one thing to focus on, one thing that will help me get through today. Anything. Please."

I scanned through my day for something that might give me relief. Waking up. Showering. Getting dressed. Driving to work. Saying good morning to coworkers. Starting a new design account. Meetings. Lunch . . . maybe.

I decided on one of the few things that still made me smile: "I'll eat a chocolate chip cookie."

I sat up and headed to the shower. I dressed myself in opaque black tights and a baggy tweed skirt suit I bought from a store I frequented that catered to affluent seniors. I tied my black hair in a tight bun at the nape of my neck and put on my wire-framed glasses and a pair of pearl earrings I had received as a wedding gift from an uncle. I was careful to look polished so no one would suspect that I was actually breaking apart, but I was also purposefully unobtrusive so as not to draw too much attention. I drove to work in my reliable silver sedan, and after lunch, I sat at a café table while I savored each sweet bite of my chocolate chip cookie, taking time to sip black coffee between each morsel. For those minutes, there was nothing else, no one to please, nothing to prove, just a cookie and me.

I

IN THE MONTHS THAT FOLLOWED, I FELT MYSELF BECOME more numb. There were muffled sounds of laughter and life bustling all around me, and yet it felt like I was submerged deep underwater, separated and hearing only the sound of my own breath and my heart slowly beating. I lived in this isolated world, sometimes comforted by the imaginary cocoon that solitude created, but mostly feeling anxious and restless for anything but the stillness. I was desperate to escape the feeling, and the longer it continued, the more I fantasized about a world where not only did I not exist, but where I had never existed at all.

The first time this thought had crossed my mind was about seven years earlier. I was lying in bed on a sunny afternoon, having come home during summer break from art college across the country with an overwhelming sense of pressure closing in on me. I didn't understand it completely—I didn't know why I felt it at all. Perhaps I could sense that I had disappointed my parents with the career I had chosen, but I also knew that I hadn't been something that I was told I was supposed to be. I simply didn't know how. Feeling like a helpless failure, I toyed with the idea of death. But I didn't want to disappoint my family even more than I felt I had already, and I imagined that suicide would be shameful and burdensome for them. I wanted to be eliminated from their memories entirely.

I pulled and straightened the blanket over my head, hiding and imagining myself disappearing.

"How perfect would it be if I never existed? I could escape all of this," I whispered, the sheets resting lightly on my face. They smelled musty and comforting, like my parents' home.

Years later, these seemingly innocent daydreams were replaced with invasive, surprising, flickering images. Every time I crossed the street, changed lanes, or drove through an intersection, I would see Mack trucks demolishing me. As I soaked in the tub, the image of my dead body in a bath of blood would appear in my mind, along with scenes of G discovering it and then having to make agonizing calls to my family.

When I was a young adult, my younger cousin C killed herself. I overheard that when her parents had found her, in a basement room, there was blood everywhere. I caught a glimpse of the room later. The white linoleum floor was spotless, and I wondered who had cleaned it. Over the years following, I continued to see the devastating impact on the entire family. I saw the light die in my uncle's eyes, never to return. I understood that C didn't foresee the pain she would cause in her family's life by ending her own, but the memory of that time and the knowledge that I would hurt those I loved if I chose to leave it were the only things holding me to life, like a leash.

But still, when the sadness was too paralyzing and all I could see and feel was my own incessant pain, I just wanted relief. "I think the best way is to take pills, painless and peaceful," I journaled one evening. "But there is always the fear of waking up and things being worse, like brain damage, paralysis. Slitting my wrists is also an option, only because I hate the idea of suffocation. But that is messy (the blood, G would have to clean it up). Hanging: not pretty; they will have too much to regret when pulling me down. I heard C took painkillers. I heard there was blood, but she did it. She was decisive, resolute and spent time saying goodbye. I could too. I could write letters."

I resolved to make a better plan, one where my family wouldn't have to find my dead body or clean up some morbid mess. My plan also needed to be foolproof; they couldn't be burdened by the consequences of the plan backfiring. And, though I figured it wouldn't be more than the pain I already felt, I didn't want it to hurt a lot.

I began my research there and Googled "painless ways to kill yourself." Diagrams, including medieval, gothic imagery flooded my screen. I clicked on a link for a forum topic: "Carbon monoxide is often not as effective as commonly believed." I educated myself on how catalytic converters decreased the levels of poison in exhaust and the increasingly popular "death by hibachi." But then I read a comment that made my body go cold.

"Don't do it, it's not worth it."

It wasn't the truth of the statement that caught me off-guard; it was the unexpectedly banal stereotype that snapped me into a different consciousness. It reminded me of all those movies where someone is trying to talk an unstable person off a building's ledge. Then it dawned on me that, in this scenario, I was the one on the edge of the cliché, and it all seemed laughable and then incredibly frightening when contrasted to the reality of how close I was to killing myself. I had to tell G.

"I looked up ways to kill myself today. I don't think that's normal."

"No. Maybe you should go talk to someone. I'm not sure I can help you."

II

A WEEK OR TWO LATER, I WALKED INTO THE THERAPIST'S office for the first time, unsure of what I would find and trying my best to seem "normal" as I filled out an intake form, smiling widely at the receptionist and exaggerating my outer composure.

Shortly afterward, I was greeted by N, a petite, soft-spoken woman. She was elegantly dressed and her thick, dark hair and fair complexion created a striking drama. She led me down a carpeted hallway to her small office, furnished with a desk, a large armchair, and a leather loveseat that seemed to slump into an overly relaxed shape.

"Sit wherever you feel most comfortable, Jackie," she said to me. It sounded rehearsed, and I realized there were people with preferences for where they sat in a room, a concept strange to me as I was accustomed to sitting wherever there was an empty spot.

She looked at me, and when her large eyes connected with mine, I noticed that they were dark, like black coffee. She smiled, and I immediately felt exposed, so I looked down and around hesitantly at the shelves of self-help books, the potted plant, and the box of tissues strategically placed beside the large armchair. I imagined the people who had cried in that chair and wondered what pained them. My eyes finally landed on a random patch of carpet, ashamed of the sadness they held in direct contrast to the peacefulness in hers.

Once we settled down opposite one another, N thanked me for coming; it took bravery to do so. I felt neither brave nor deserving of the compliment. She handed me a form on a clipboard and, with an accent I still cannot pinpoint to this day, she asked me to sign a simple contract: to refrain from suicide during the time we worked together. I stopped to contemplate the things that might happen if I chose to stay alive. The thing is, I wasn't afraid of death; whether or not to kill myself was just another important decision to be made, with relative detachment. To me, it was much like deciding whether to take that lucrative job in a distant city; it was just a logical weighing of pros and cons.

I will end my suffering.

But my family may be traumatized.

They say you don't feel pain in heaven.
But if I kill myself, they say I'll go to hell.
I will no longer be an emotional burden to G.
But I will miss having children one day.

If I did feel any fear in that moment in N's office, it was of being left without a choice to kill myself if it ever became too unbearable to live. But I agreed to the terms for one year, at which point N and I would reassess. After all, I figured that I had nothing to lose and could always go back to suicide if I found nothing else more effective.

The time I spent in N's little office over the next year was a mixture of many things: controlled, confused, triumphant, slow, intense, curious, sad. Most of the time I felt as if I had no idea where I was and if I was getting better at all. I wanted to see results fast, and after some weeks I became bitter at the irritatingly slow pace of improvement. I resented role-playing, annoyed by the make-believe when I had "real problems" to solve. I would walk away wondering if I was just wasting my time trying to live. I remember feeling embarrassed when she suggested that I draw out my feelings on large sheets of paper with multicolored pastels, which felt impotent and uninformative. It was no use, I pre-analyzed the meaning behind every line and shape before I placed it on paper, a lingering skill from my many years of art school critiques. I presumed that hard, dark scribbles most likely signified some repressed anger, or a bright green blotch would communicate hidden hope, and it all just felt . . . stupid. And I felt even more stupid for needing the exercise.

During each session, N would ask me how I felt. I was never really certain. The feelings were cloudy and evasive and often I would answer with a question, tiptoeing to see if I got it right. "Bad? Maybe?"

One day, she pulled out a photocopied sheet of paper, on it a grid of simply-drawn cartoon faces. A smiling face, and under it written "happy." Another with an open mouth, pointed eyebrows, and strained eyes: "angry." One with tears falling from the eyes and a downturned mouth: "sad." I searched through the faces trying to find one that looked most similar to my own and settled tentatively on one with a curled mouth and a furrowed brow: "confused." But I had no words. I was so thoroughly disconnected from myself that I didn't even have the ability to express the most elementary emotions. When I saw this, I knew it was unhealthy and I wondered if I was so far gone that I couldn't even be helped at all.

The confusion came and went like tides, washing in and out for over five years. At times, what was once difficult to grasp became instinctive, which encouraged me to continue. But then I would become confused again, disheartened, as if the progress I had made was only something I had imagined. I began discovering what gave me joy, like a perfect hamburger (medium-rare with a good bun and iceberg lettuce), scattering seeds for little birds in my garden, or a line of pewter sequins on a new wool skirt decorated with bright fuchsia and orange flowers. As I gave myself the space to exist, to have things to like, it occurred to me that I also had dislikes, that I deserved to feel delight and feel hurt as well. I had been taught that feeling hurt was a burden to others, and that I had likely done something to deserve it. So I began fighting, mostly against this ancient idea passed on to me, for permission to feel angry for the first time since I was a child.

III

SOME MORNINGS BEFORE WORK, I WOULD SIMPLY LIE IN BED, lifeless, and some days G would wrap me up in a blanket, lift me onto a chair and say lovingly, "Today, just do the minimum. Just do things that will help you respect yourself." On other mornings, my depression was too heavy even for him to bear, and I could feel him moving away from me so that he could breathe himself.

One winter afternoon, I lay in bed crying. I was exhausted from pushing so hard, feeling again as if I was getting nowhere, ever. I prayed to God, asking why it had to be so painful, so hard, and an incredible shrieking rose up from out of me, an anger at being forced to live. I screamed and sobbed uncontrollably for many minutes, clenching my fists and finding nowhere to punch except my own thighs and head to release my resentment. G opened the door.

"What's the matter?" he asked quietly, his concern mixed faintly with exasperation.

"I can't do this anymore."

"What?" he stayed in the doorway, watching me.

"Everything!" I yelled. "Haven't I been through enough already? Hasn't God given me enough shit to deal with? Haven't I worked hard enough? I'm so fucking tired!" My words descended into a long sob. "I just want to be happy. Why is God doing this to me? When will I just get a fucking break? I've done my best, I've paid my dues, when will this end?" G was silent.

He watched as I buried my face in the blankets, using them to wipe my face. Then he spoke. "Life doesn't owe you a thing, Jackie. It doesn't owe you happiness. And I don't want to be insensitive, but all the pain you feel, you've probably created it yourself. You are not a victim; you're being a spoiled brat. Every choice you make has a consequence, and you have to deal with it. The pain is there to teach you what you need to change. You can stop making the same decisions every day and expecting something different. You have a choice here." I stopped crying immediately. I was stunned. His words slapped me back into a rational state.

"Why haven't you ever said that to me before? Wait . . . have you?" I wondered aloud, my eyes darted back and forth as I searched through past conversations. G didn't answer. *Maybe he did, but I wasn't ready to understand it. Or was I so afraid to hear the truth that I chose to continue drowning in my own self-pity?*

"I have a choice here?" I looked at him, confused.

"Like with your mom. You want for her to be a different person than who she is. Each time you see her, you try to change her. Afterward, you come home upset that she's done the exact same thing she has done every single time. And then the next time you see her, you try the same thing with the same result. You can't change her, or anyone. You can only change yourself," he explained. I still didn't understand.

"So what? I just have to keep being hurt by everyone around me?" I retorted.

"Think of your mom as a lion. You want her to be a dog, so each time you see her, you try to pet her, but lions bite. Respect that a lion will bite, and change your expectations and the way you interact with it," he continued.

"Lions are lions, and dogs are dogs . . ." I began to understand.

"And if you don't like getting bitten, you don't have to pet the lion. If you find yourself in a situation you don't like, you also don't have to stay. That's your choice."

Examples began to cycle though my mind, of the times I was bitten, the times I stayed, not knowing I had a choice. I began to see just how true it was, and how far this idea that I was a victim had spread into every detail of my life. A hazy veil began to lift.

"And if you like something, do it again. That's your choice too," G added.

I let that thought circle in my mind for a long while.

IV

PRECISELY A YEAR AFTER WE FIRST BEGAN MEETING EACH other every week, N checked in with me.

"Jackie, would you like to continue?"

It was time to choose again whether I wanted to live. Even though I had begun to take control of my life over the course of my time with N, making big and small decisions for myself—how I spent alone time on weekends, changing the way I interacted with lions, choosing where I wanted to sit in a room, placing a flower or two at my desk, buying a beautiful mug for my morning coffee—it was a new skill that I sometimes struggled with. I regularly stumbled and found myself exasperated by the effort it took to remember that I had a choice in everything. I was undoing a habit that was deeply entrenched in me. So each morning I still reminded myself of the contract I'd signed, and then made the choice to be alive.

Each time I felt discouraged, when I couldn't see any end to the struggling, I would reach into my back pocket to feel for my "get out of jail free card." It was always there, the suicide fallback plan, reassuring and comforting me in the risk to live. I sat on the decision, not wanting to let go of the feeling of safety I had created with the idea of death.

As I was driving home one day, lost in my own thoughts and feeling particularly defeated, I instinctively reached for the comfortable idea of death to soothe myself. "I could just kill myself if this gets any worse." The thought came like a reflex.

I stopped the fantasy. I saw that I was perching on a fence, refusing to commit to life or death, living but not fully dead or fully alive. I was neither getting the relief or freedom that I believed there was in death, nor was I getting the beauty of living wholeheartedly. Instead, I was struggling with the disadvantages of both: the fantasy of death had become a crutch, and if I continued to use it, I would never discover how strong I had become. And if I refused to take a chance, if I held myself back in the search to find happiness because I was too scared of failing, or worse, finding at the end of it that it didn't exist to begin with . . . then I would indeed create this very fate anyway. I would never find the happiness I had been working for, and it would all be a waste. For so long I had dreamt of dying, to dispose of a life I despised in so many ways. But if I were to throw my life away anyway, I thought, maybe I could waste it living, doing whatever the fuck I wanted, however the fuck I wanted to. I would have been dead anyway.

So, then, I made the choice to throw away the life I despised, and to waste my life living, and to never entertain the idea of death again.

CHOCOLATE CHIP COOKIES

This recipe has been adapted from the well-known recipe from the New York Times. *I had tried many recipes obsessively over the years and narrowed them down to three favorites: this is one I still make often when I want an ooey gooey cookie that is chewy in the center with crisp, caramelized edges.*

FOR THE VANILLA MALDON SALT
1 vanilla bean
½ cup (125 ml) Maldon salt

Split the vanilla bean lengthwise and scrape out the seeds in the center with the back of a small paring knife. Place the husk and the seeds in a resealable container with the Maldon salt and mix gently with a fork to combine. Infuse for at least 36 hours at room temperature. You can leave the husk in the salt indefinitely to continue infusing, storing at room temperature. The salt will just pick up more of the vanilla scent and flavors the longer it is left to mingle. When the cookies are warm and just out of the oven, sprinkle a pinch onto the top of each one.

A NOTE ON THE USES OF THE SALT: This recipe makes more than you might need for the cookies, but I like to keep some on hand at all times. Vanilla salt is perfect for finishing dishes like seared scallops or on almost any kind of sweet such as brownies, cakes, cookies, and caramel ice cream.

FOR THE COOKIES
2½ sticks (10 oz/284 g) unsalted butter, room temperature
1 cup plus 2 tbsp (8 oz/227 g) granulated sugar
1¼ cups (10 oz/285 g) light brown sugar
2 tsp (10 ml) vanilla extract (I prefer Nielsen-Massey)
2 large eggs

3¾ cups (16.5 oz/468 g) all-purpose flour

1½ tsp (7.5 ml) fine sea salt

1½ tsp (7.5 ml) baking powder

1¼ tsp (6 ml) baking soda

10 oz (285 g) bittersweet chocolate fèves
(I prefer Valrhona Alpaco; see note below)

10 oz (285 g) milk chocolate fèves (I prefer Valrhona Jivara)

Cream the butter and sugars in a large bowl or in the bowl of a stand mixer, until lighter in color and texture. Add the vanilla extract and eggs to the butter mixture and mix on medium speed until fully incorporated, scraping down the sides of the bowl as needed.

Slowly add the flour, salt, baking powder, and baking soda, mixing on low speed until just combined. There should be large streaks of flour still remaining. Add the chocolate fèves and mix briefly until just incorporated.

Cover the dough with plastic wrap or place in an airtight container, and then refrigerate it for 48 hours. Aging the dough melds the flavors and creates nutty caramel notes that won't develop otherwise.

When you are ready to bake the cookies, preheat the oven to 350°F. Remove the dough from the refrigerator about 30 minutes before scooping to soften it slightly. Line 2 sheet trays with parchment paper. Scoop balls of dough about 2 inches in diameter and place them about 2 inches apart on the trays. You can use a heaping #30 (1 fluid ounce) scoop if you have one.

Bake for about 15 minutes or until the cookies are browned and caramelized along the edges and centers are just set.

Top each cookie with a sprinkling of the vanilla-infused Maldon salt, about ¼ teaspoon. Cool on trays for 2 minutes and transfer to a rack to cool completely, or eat warm. Repeat with remaining cookie dough. Keep in an airtight container for up to 3 days.

A NOTE ON MEASUREMENTS: I have given measurements here in both volume and weight. However, I find I get the most consistent results using weight. A kitchen scale is reasonably affordable and you will find that it makes baking and cleanup much faster and easier.

A NOTE ON THE CHOCOLATE: While it is harder to find fèves (discs of chocolate) than chocolate chips, there is a distinct difference in the resulting cookie—the chocolate layers in the cookie in a way that does not quite happen with regular chocolate chips.

MAKES 30–36 COOKIES.

PORK AND CHIVE DUMPLINGS

{1921–2014}

Every truth has four corners:

AS A TEACHER I GIVE YOU ONE

CORNER, AND IT IS FOR YOU

TO FIND THE OTHER THREE.

Confucius

I WASN'T RAISED ON CASSEROLES AND GRILLED CHEESE sandwiches. Unlike most of the kids I grew up with, the concept of Ants on a Log utterly confused me. My classmates came to elementary school toting cheddar snack packs and carrot sticks with ranch dip, snacks that were completely foreign to me. I envied them because they were "normal" and I, nibbling on my pork floss with dried seaweed, wasn't. So out of a curiosity for a culture I felt alien to, I used my hard-earned allowance to buy peanut butter, celery, and raisins to recreate a recipe dictated to me by a seven-year-old: "You take peanut butter, stick it in the middle of the celery, and put raisins on top, like ants . . . on a log." Obviously.

To my all-encompassing delight, the celery, with its refreshing crunch and the way it made a convenient cradle; the sweet, chewy raisins; and the unctuous, fragrant peanut butter, were all, frankly, heavenly. I ate Ants on a Log obsessively for weeks afterward.

Before this revelation, my experiences with after-school snacks were of ethereal scallion crêpes, so wide they hung over the rim of our largest dinner plates, or whole-wheat buns, piping hot from the bamboo steamer. I would methodically peel the dried bamboo leaf from the underside and cut the bun into slices. Wholly un-Chinese, I also slathered it with pats of butter so generous that they would melt on the hot bread and drip down my fingers. Even at a young age I knew butter was a beautiful substance.

I was very lucky to have my grandmother live with me as a child. Ah Lau or Lau, as we called her, was a talented cook with a critical palate, trained in the school of necessity from raising her nine hungry children. She would not have known Ants on a Log.

My large family consisted of my parents, my grandparents, two uncles, an aunt, two cousins, and my sister. We lived snugly, cooking and eating together at the dinner table every night. Weekends were reserved for grocery shopping as a group in Chinatown. I followed the adults, both mesmerized and repelled by the dried seahorses in herbal shops, picking at bins of dried lily bulbs and overhearing consultations on matters such as how to pick the sweetest watermelon. (It should "hit back" when you slap it with your palm.)

I

LAU CARED FOR ME WITH TENDERNESS AND PRACTICALITY, and she raised me with food. If I close my eyes, I can still feel the staccato rhythm of a hefty Chinese cleaver chopping vegetables on a butcher's block as she and my mom made dinner. I would often watch from the side, trying to absorb all the smells and wanting to know what came next, but staying well out of the way.

Lau also taught me my first lessons on food. As she mumbled aloud to herself, she dropped hints and tips like a breadcrumb trail that I listened to as I played beside her: how to balance the flavors and textures of noodles and soups; how to smell saltiness in a dish without tasting it. I felt moments suspend as I touched dough to sense how much water it needed to make perfect dumplings. I learned that chopsticks bubble in oil when the wok has come to temperature, and that only the thinnest streams of egg will create wisps like smoke when dropped into corn soup. I was surrounded by food all the time, and I absorbed as much of it as I could.

I was amazed at how Lau's blunt hands were equally adroit at using an embroidery needle on fine fabric as they were with a cleaver cutting thick bones. But of all the seemingly impossible feats she performed, as a toddler I marveled most at how she could tie me onto her back with nothing more than a bedsheet. It was like magic how the fabric folded so my little body hung there carefree with my cheek against her back, drifting off to the sound of her beating heart as she bustled in the kitchen.

II

ONE SUMMER WHEN I WAS ABOUT TEN, WE DROVE UP the coast of British Columbia for a family camping trip. We spent a whole afternoon digging clams together on the beach. My parents showed me how to look for little air holes in the sand, a sign that the clams were hidden deep beneath them. After we had filled several buckets, my parents found the only Chinese restaurant in the rural town of Campbell River and asked for the clams to be sautéed in a savory black bean sauce. When enormous plates were placed on the lazy Susan in front of us, I ate and ate until I couldn't possibly hold any more, slurping each shell with its driblet of pungent sauce and little plum of flesh, gradually piling the empty ornate shells on my little plate, but keeping the prettier ones to one side.

The following morning, our car packed up with our summer belongings, we headed back toward the city. After an hour of driving in our sky-blue minivan, my mom noticed something out of the ordinary in a ditch along the highway. My father pulled the van over, got out, and walked briskly toward the trench. He knelt down and picked a blade of green growing from it, and then returned to the car and said to my mom in Chinese, "It's watercress."

The entire family was forced out of the van, given black garbage bags, and directed to pick watercress. We picked for hours along the highway until not only did we have more than we could realistically eat, but there was none left to be found. After that we ate watercress for many days, but I didn't mind much, as I liked the bitter taste of it sautéed with garlic and its stringy softness in soup.

III

FOR ALMOST EVERY SPECIAL OCCASION THROUGHOUT MY life—Christmases, Thanksgivings, birthdays, and especially each Chinese New Year—my family made dumplings. Come to think of it, we made dumplings for many regular occasions as well. My family had roots in northern China, known for being the best cooks, and dumplings were our specialty. We made all sorts of dumplings: pork and chive, fish and cilantro, vermicelli and wood ear mushroom for the years in high school when I decided I was a vegetarian.

Making dumplings was a day-long affair that started at the markets, where sui choy, meat, shrimp, chives, and cilantro were bought. Then the entire family would gather in the kitchen, half hotly debating whether the dough needed more water, the other half deep in a fury of chopping. The meat was always cut by hand, never pre-ground, as the slight inconsistencies gave a better texture to the filling. The shrimp were peeled and the sui choy was finely diced, heavily salted in a bowl and squeezed of its excess moisture, using the palms as a muscly press. After all the ingredients were thrown into a bowl, seasoned, and whisked using a bundle of chopsticks, the entire family, men and women, would surround the filling, smelling it, inspecting it, and arguing about whether there was the right amount of salt. When I put my nose into the bowl, it was aromatic with mingling scents of toasted sesame oil and green onions stinging my nostrils.

"It's enough!" someone would say.

"How would you know? You always make everything so bland!" someone else would rebut.

With a coy smile, another would pick a side. "I think your nose is just for decoration; you can barely smell a thing."

"Who needs to smell if I can taste better than anyone?"

After a few more playful jabs, my grandmother would chime in with the final word: "It's fine." And then we'd start.

As a young child, I would watch this production of dumplings intently for hours, hoping that one day they would let me help, too. They would roll the dough into long snake-like ropes that wiggled on the floured table. Then, as though they were swiftly tearing off the snake's head, they would pull little bits of dough off until they reached its tail, each piece pressed with the base of the palm into a little round. Two others would rock slim rolling pins over the edge of each round, turning it as they moved until it was thin and smooth like a sand dollar. As the wrappers were made, others dropped in dollops of filling, and stretched the ends together. In one orchestrated movement, thumbs and fingers would wrap tightly around the package to form frilly crowns of dough atop plump bellies.

My favorite part was right at the end. Nothing went to waste: with the leftover dough they would make flaky scallion pancakes. I preferred when my uncle made the pancakes because he would add little salty gems of Chinese bacon, making them doubly delicious.

When the table was finally set, we ate rounds of dumplings, steaming hot and dipped in black vinegar mixed with minced raw garlic alongside. The table also held dishes of pig ears braised in soy sauce, cucumber jellyfish salad, fried chicken wings, and soup made of dried oysters and hair moss. Conversations were always loud and rose even noisier with boisterous laughing or debating, and at the end of the evening I was always full, satiated.

SHORTLY AFTER I RETURNED FROM PARIS, LAU SUDDENLY became ill. I walked into her hospital room, apprehensive of what I might see. I had been so heartbroken by my cousin C's death. I remembered how strange and watery C's body looked in her coffin, a sharp contrast to the sparkling soul secured with vibrant eyes and virile black hair she had when she was alive.

Lau was in her nineties, and the doctors prepared us for the inevitable. My family explained death to me as if I were a child and referred to it as "falling asleep" in order to cushion the pain, like my heartsick aunt did when C died. But in my aunt's case, she had done it to soothe herself and not me.

For weeks, I stayed by my grandmother's side, holding her hands still in mine as she deliriously made sewing motions and mumbled to herself about things that happened long before I was born. Forced into poverty during World War II, she had worked as a seamstress after immigrating to Hong Kong, and so these movements, like deeply trodden paths, resurfaced in her unconscious state. Whenever her eyes opened, she would recognize few people, instead seeing in us loved ones from her memories. She remembered me; I don't know why. And when she was restless or anxious from hallucinations, I would place my thumb in the little space between her eyebrows and stroke her smooth skin until her eyes closed to peaceful sleep.

Day after day I did this, along with many other members of my family, silently and patiently waiting for death to take Lau. And then one day, she opened her eyes. I could see that she was lucid. She began to speak again with that sassy, devil-may-care attitude. She repeated the exact same things she'd said to me since I was little: she told me to cut my hair and then wondered why I had such a dark tan. She explained that only peasants working in fields have dark tans—which I guess was true in China when she was young.

I went home and made her a chicken ginseng soup, which she refused to eat, as her appetite hadn't returned. The next day as I was putting spoonfuls into her mouth, she looked up at me with a characteristic scowl and said, "Why is this so bitter?" I hadn't realized the effect that reboiling the soup had on its pure flavor. Lau had just come back from the brink of death, and she was still critiquing my cooking.

V

AFTER LAU LEFT THE HOSPITAL, WE QUICKLY DEVELOPED a daily routine. I would arrive at the seniors' home in time to take her out of bed, help her get dressed, and wheel her out to the common room for breakfast. I would feed her oatmeal mixed with warm milk and scrambled eggs with toast and jam. She would complain about the thickened water she had to drink, and I knew she longed for a cup of hot Chinese tea.

As I fed her, I would exercise my diminishing Chinese and relay all the gossip I had heard about anyone. At times I would embellish the story if I knew it would make her laugh.

This went on for many months: me taking her for walks and engaging her mind. It gave me an excuse to be out of the house. The tension between G and me had escalated, and our marriage was nearly broken. By this point we had barely spoken to each other for months, not for lack of wanting to—we just didn't know what else to say. I didn't tell Lau, but maybe she could sense something was wrong, as she would give me ancient marriage advice that seemed to have emerged from some time capsule.

"When will you have children?" she would ask daily, forgetting our conversation from the day before.

"He told me he no longer wants to have kids. What am I to do?"

"Just 'remove the block' and have one anyway. He will love it all the same when it comes out."

I laughed. "I can't do that. It's different nowadays."

"Then what will you do without children?"

"Maybe I won't have them."

"Crazy," she dismissed.

I would then ask her about my grandfather, Lau Ye, and how they met. She told me that after her marriage was arranged at sixteen, she snuck into a neighboring village to spy on him. She needed to know if he was ugly or handsome.

"Were you scared?" I asked.

"Of what?"

"That he would be mean, or that you would hate him."

"I had no choice, so why think of those things?"

And day after day, we had this same conversation, until one day I changed my response. It had become so clear that with G, with or without children, I would never be able to live the life I desperately wanted—my own. I had grown so much, so far away from him, and I knew the only way to bridge the gap was to move toward him and away from myself. But I didn't want to lose myself again, and unlike Lau, I had a choice.

"When will you have children?"

"I'm going to leave him."

VI

WHEN MY GRANDFATHER, LAU YE, DIED OF CANCER, I WAS eighteen and living in Toronto, a fine arts student pretending to be an adult for the first time. I was angry with him for something I'd heard he had done in the past and refused to go back to Vancouver for his funeral. It was an honest anger, but now I see that I only felt it so passionately because I was young and didn't have the maturity to see that life is ambiguously made up of elegant grays, and that nothing truly exists outside of compassion and people bumping into each other, trying so hard to figure it out themselves.

The night he died, I had a dream so clear that I never forgot it. In the dream, instead of using words, I remember he took me to beautiful places, each scene more overwhelming and breathtaking than the last. At the end, we stood on a beach watching the sunset in silence. The sky glowed with vermilion, coral, copper, rose, and lilac. He held my hand, and I knew he was helping me let go of the past and giving me the gift of a good goodbye.

VII

AH LAU WENT IN AND OUT OF THE HOSPITAL, IN AND out of death for a couple years. Each time, I would rush to her, running as fast as my legs could move, even though it felt as if I was fighting through water. Family from around the world would fly in and surround her bed with mournful looks and naked sobs, and I would arrive, panting, my chest burning. I'd wait by her bed for days. She would come to life again, but then we would watch every other part of her body and mind decline into death.

Each time, I held her hand and said goodbye; and each time I let her go, my heart shattered into many pieces. Then one day after she had recovered from the brink of death again, my heart just couldn't—it couldn't break anymore. So I walked away and left her before she had left me. I stopped visiting her, stopped seeing her, and in my mind, I pretended she was gone because I couldn't bring myself to say goodbye again.

The night she actually died, I drove to the hospital more slowly than usual, knowing she would be gone before I arrived. I walked up to her darkened room, along the shadowed hallways, lit by the odd flickering fluorescent light. When I saw her in her bed, she was departed, her eyes closed and mouth agape, my aunt still holding her hand. I walked into a dark corner and cried.

Each time someone close to me dies, I see them in my dreams shortly after just like Lau Ye, to say I'm sorry and to say goodbye. With Lau, I waited night after night for her to come, but she never came, so I cried for that too.

PORK AND CHIVE DUMPLINGS

*This is my family recipe, which has evolved over too many generations
to count. We are still trying to perfect them. This recipe is a large one, so I
recommend getting your friends and family involved, or feel free to halve the
recipe. It makes enough for a large feast with some left over to freeze for later.*

FOR THE DOUGH

480 g all-purpose white flour, plus more for dusting

750 g cake and pastry flour

710 g of water

(Slightly less or more water may be needed to achieve a smooth
dough that is soft and pliable but not sticky after it is kneaded.
It should feel like a baby's bottom when you poke it.)

Mix both flours in a large bowl with clean fingers. Add ¾ of the water and mix
and knead the dough with your hands until it becomes a dry, shaggy mass.
Add the remainder of the water to the drier parts of the flour mixture and
continue kneading it in the bowl until the dough just comes together into
a ball, the flour has been incorporated, and the bowl is relatively clean.
Transfer to a table and knead just until the dough seems evenly hydrated
and there are no more pockets of dry flour or wet dough. Do not overmix,
though: it should not be smooth but rough-looking. Cover with plastic wrap
and allow to sit at room temperature for at least 2 hours to rest. My family
makes this in the morning and lets it rest while we go to the market for fresh
ingredients. If you leave the dough longer or overnight, knead it again, as
the gluten will have relaxed too much and there will not be enough structure to hold the filling properly. If you notice the dough is too stretchy or soft,
re-knead it until it firms up.

FOR THE FILLING

The process of making the filling is divided into 3 parts. The results from
each part will be mixed together before filling and technically, you could
combine them all at once, but my mother swears that the flavor is much
better when each part is done separately. She also says that it ends up being

the perfect marinating time for each component when it is done separately, since the ingredients in Part A must be marinated longer than B and C.

PART A

670 g organic pork butt
(or Boston butt, which comes from above the shoulder blade)

670 g organic pork shoulder
(which is below the butt, on the front leg quarter)

40 g light soy sauce

40 g chicken stock

4 g toasted sesame oil

1 tsp fine sea salt

½ tsp pepper

Chop the pork into a coarse minced texture by hand. My mom uses a cleaver on a butcher's block, cutting the meat into thin slices, then into small cubes. She removes any tendons. She then uses the cleaver to pass over the meat several times, folding the mince onto itself to ensure it is all evenly chopped. Chopping the meat by hand gives the filling a better texture when cooked.

Place the meat in a bowl and marinate it by adding the stock, soy sauce, sesame oil, salt, and pepper. Mix well with 4 chopsticks used as a whisk and set aside in the refrigerator for at least 45 minutes.

PART B

645 g tiger prawns, peeled and deveined

10 g light soy sauce

6 g toasted sesame oil

4 g grated ginger, including juice

3 g Shaoxing wine

½ tsp fine sea salt

¼ tsp pepper

Cut the tiger prawns into ¼-inch pieces and marinate them in a bowl with the soy sauce, sesame oil, ginger, wine, salt, and pepper. Mix and set aside in the refrigerator for at least 30 minutes.

A NOTE ON SHAOXING WINE: This is a common ingredient found in any Chinese grocery store, but sherry cooking wine can be used as a substitute in a pinch.

PART C

765 g Chinese chives

225 g scallions

90 g cilantro

425 g zucchini

235 g chicken stock

30 g vegetable oil

27 g light soy sauce

2 tsp toasted sesame oil

2 tsp fine sea salt

Chop the chives, scallions, and cilantro very finely and place in a large mixing bowl. Cut the zucchini into a 1/16-inch dice and add to the vegetable mixture. Add the stock, vegetable oil, soy sauce, sesame oil, and salt. Combine the marinated pork from Part A and the shrimp from Part B. Mix this very well using the chopstick whisk or by hand. Set aside until you are ready to assemble the dumplings.

A NOTE ON CHINESE CHIVES: You can substitute regular chives for these, however Chinese chives, which you can find at any Chinese grocery store, are sturdier, and will have a different consistency after being cooked.

A NOTE ON SOY SAUCE: There is a wide variety of soy sauce out there. It would be preferable to use a Chinese light soy sauce, but a regular soy sauce from the supermarket would be a good substitute if you can't find light soy sauce. Just be sure not to buy a dark version, as the flavor will be too intense.

½ cup black vinegar

2 tbsp toasted sesame oil

Mix together.

A NOTE ON BLACK VINEGAR: This might be a difficult ingredient to find. To make your own substitution, mix equal parts white vinegar and light soy sauce.

TO MAKE THE DUMPLINGS

Cut the ball of dough into 4 equal pieces and cover the bowl with plastic wrap to keep it from drying out.

Knead 1 piece of dough until smooth on a floured surface; we use an old wooden board that has been passed down for generations. Cut the dough into 4 strips, and roll each one into a rope about ¾ inch thick, lightly flouring the counter to keep it from sticking.

Cut or rip the rope into half-inch pieces and flatten each with the palm of your hand to create little discs about 1½ inches in diameter.

Using a Chinese rolling pin (or a food safe dowel about 1 inch in diameter) roll out each dough piece into little rounds, as thin as a sheet of linen at the edges and a little thicker in the center. They will have a diameter of about 2½ inches.

Place 1–2 tablespoons of filling in the center of a round. Pinch opposite sides together firmly to create a half-moon dumpling shape. You can use your fingers to pinch different pleated patterns into the dough, but my family prefers a quicker, rustic style that is simply squeezed between the inside thumb and the side of the index finger. As you create the dumplings, place them on a floured sheet pan so they don't stick together.

Bring a large pot of water to a rolling boil. It must be the largest pot you have because the dumplings will need room to move around. Drop the dumplings in the water and swirl them around with a spoon. Cover and wait until the water boils over, and then stir again. Cover and wait once more until the water boils over, and then, using a slotted spoon, remove the dumplings to a serving dish. Serve hot with black vinegar and sesame oil dipping sauce.

A NOTE ON FREEZING DUMPLINGS: Dumplings can be frozen for up to 1 month; just add a few more minutes to the cooking time when cooking frozen dumplings. To cook frozen dumplings, bring a large pot of water to a rolling boil, drop the dumplings in the water, and swirl the dumplings in the water with a spoon. Cover and wait until the water boils over, and then add ¾ cup of cold water and swirl the water again. Cover and wait until the water boils over again. Add another ¾ cup of cold water, swirl and cover. Once the water boils over again, the dumplings are ready.

A NOTE ON THE MEASUREMENTS: This recipe requires the precision of a scale, unless you have the cooking intuition of a Chinese grandmother. Volume measurements would not be suitable for most of the ingredients and so we, as a family, decided not to include them. Where volume measurements are indicated, this would have been the most precise form of measurement.

MAKES 250–300 DUMPLINGS.

CARROT CAKE WITH CREAM CHEESE FROSTING

{1985–1992}

IT IS SAFE TO SAY

THAT WHEN THE WATER BOILS,

AS IT SURELY WILL,

given enough heat under it,

IT IS READY.

M. F. K. Fisher, How to Cook a Wolf,
"How to Boil Water"

I HAVE MANY VAGUE AND SCATTERED MEMORIES OF when I was two or three years old. They are short, just glimpses, and, come to think of it, I'm not even sure how accurate they are.

When my sister was at school during the day, the house always seemed very quiet. My mom would sleep a lot, her room quite dark. It seemed normal to me, but I remember spending a lot of time trying to wake her up and a lot of time playing by myself. Many years later, when I was about fourteen years old, she told me a story.

One day she was lying in her bed, in that same dark room. She told me she had taken medication, I think a painkiller for an injury, and had a severe allergic reaction to it. She recalls slowly floating to the ceiling, seeing her own lifeless body below her. Outside the bedroom, emanating from past the hallway, was the warmest and most pleasant light. She told me that it was so inviting she began to float toward it, like a reflex, because she wanted so much to be surrounded by it.

But all of a sudden she glanced back and remembered my sister and me, her babies. She heard the voices of friends and family members talking as if they were at her funeral. They said how sad it was that we were left without a mother to raise us; they worried about our futures and how we would fare. She looked once more at the light, longingly, but then forced her way against it, back to the darkness of the room, and lay onto her own body again.

Her eyes opened immediately, and she crawled across the floor struggling to get to a telephone to call for help. She told me that she couldn't bear the thought of leaving us, and so she chose to live that day and to never leave.

I

AROUND THE SAME TIME, MY MOTHER PROBABLY READ some article about the evil effects of sugar on a child's brain development and vowed to protect me from all sweet dangers. And so she did, with love, fierce piety, and an iron fist. In our home, Gobstoppers or gummy worms would never cross lips, no mouths were stained in freezie-colored hues, and my food pyramid had no room for sugar highs or lows. You might wonder how these kinds of restrictions affect a child's development into adulthood. Well, taking me as a case study, it appears that the pendulum swings far, and the child eventually takes sweet revenge and opens a bakery.

When I accompanied my mother to the butcher, I would longingly fiddle with the chocolate coins displayed in baskets alongside the canned artichokes and anchovies. While she paid for our week's worth of luncheon meats, the cashier would carefully place in my hand a single candy with patterns of bright fruits printed on its wrapper. Each time, my jaw dropped and my heart pounded with the excitement and disbelief of a lottery winner, but just as I closed my fingers around it, my mother would pluck the candy from my little palm and return it to the cashier. I would be speechless.

My older sister didn't have much more luck than I did. Over dinner three decades later, we traded stories of our sugar deprivation as if piecing together a common alien abduction experience. We realized that both of us had scrounged through the pantry drinking vanilla extract in a desperate search for anything that might taste like candy.

Over time, through torturous trial and error, we discovered two ways to get mom to let us eat sweets. The first was to ask her at a strategically timed moment. Since she worked evening shifts at the time, we noted that she was vulnerable and compliant during her afternoon nap. In a sleepy daze, she would say yes to anything, including opening the boxes of chocolates she reserved as future "regifts." She would awake with a vague recollection of having agreed to something, and being a fair mother, we would escape discipline each time.

I, thankfully, had the maturity to understand at the age of six or seven that no supportive mother could deny a child wanting to learn, so as a second ploy, I began teaching myself to bake. It was never discussed nor did I ask permission; I simply rode my little red bike to the library for cookbooks, spending hours leafing through recipes and then using my ten-dollar-a-week allowance to buy ingredients. I was like a prisoner walking out the front door, the guards helpless to stop me.

I had only watched my mother bake on a few occasions, and being a sensible child, I knew that when learning new things, one must start slowly. So I started with recipes from a coil-bound cookbook we had at home, one that my elementary school had created as a fundraising effort. I was particularly drawn to recipes marked with a little drawing of a chef's hat labeled "junior chef," tasks easy enough for someone as young as I to tackle successfully. I stood at the tall kitchen counter by myself, choosing very deliberately which recipe to begin with. The one for peanut butter drops looked simple enough. I liked peanut butter, and this recipe had just four ingredients: sugar, egg, vanilla, and peanut butter. And so I began, preheating the oven, pouring the perfect amount of sugar into a large mixing bowl. I held my breath. One egg, tapped lightly on the side of the bowl, and I managed to leave out any fragments of shell. I filled measuring cups with sticky, smooth peanut butter, and added a final slip of vanilla. With a large spoon, I mashed the ingredients until they came together into a smooth, tawny paste.

One by one, I rolled tender little balls between my palms and lined them up obediently on a buttered tray. After a few minutes in the oven, watching them grow through the hazy window in the door, I smelled them, hot, caramel, nutty, sweet, and my mouth watered.

When I was sure they were done, looking for all the signs of a cookie I wanted to eat, the golden edges especially, I carefully pulled the hot pan out of the oven and rested it on top of the stove. Once they were cool enough to touch with my fingers, I picked one up and bit into it. The sweet-scented nuttiness immediately melted on my tongue, held together by the soft fragrance of vanilla. They were good. I smiled and then proceeded to eat the better part of half of them before anyone came home.

I grew more confident over the following weeks, and moved on to "kitchen sink" cookies: a chewy chocolate chip oatmeal cookie with a hint of cinnamon, shredded coconut, nuts, and even potato chips added to the batter—essentially everything. I then worked my way through the hot milk sponge cake, mouthing the recipes quietly to myself. I discovered that keeping a clean kitchen and putting things away as I went along made the process easier and that too much marshmallow in a Rice Krispie square made the Rice Krispies less crispy. Everything I made tasted delicious, and being in the kitchen felt quite natural. Without anyone's guidance, I seemed to innately know what kind of molasses to buy at the grocery store or how many chocolate chips a cookie could hold without falling apart.

It was an ideal solitary world for me to explore. I was incredibly shy outside of the home, plagued by insecurities about many things, most of which was the fear that I was stupid. Like many Asian immigrant families I've known, our family believed that being scholastically talented was of the utmost importance. It was considered the only valuable skill because they thought it was the only safe path to financial security, which in their minds meant happiness for my sister and me. But since I showed no aptitude for academics, especially compared to others in my extended family who had excelled in school, I was dismissed as "stupid" and "useless."

I felt constant guilt for being a disappointment to my family, and I felt hopeless to change my fate. So, most of the time, I thought it best not to give anyone reason to confirm my stupidity further by staying as quiet and neutral as possible, refraining from giving opinions or putting up my hand. I spent most of my energy figuring out how to be invisible at school, so I was often alone or with just one friend. Since my parents were so busy, I found that as long as I stayed out of trouble, I was free to play in the depths of my own world, exploring my imagination, drawing everything— including drawings of drawings—sewing clothes for my dolls, creating designs for dresses I longed to wear, and baking anything I wanted to eat.

I I

EVENTUALLY I HAD A FATEFUL BRUSH WITH BLUEBERRY muffins that left me feeling wholly disappointed in myself. I began as I usually did, reading out all the ingredients so as not to find myself stuck halfway through. I measured, poured, and mixed, verbalizing each step aloud with a maternal authority, making believe I was a cooking show host like my favorites Julia Child or Madhur Jaffrey. I carefully lined the dark metal muffin pan with pleated papers in pale tints of pink, blue, yellow, and green. I scooped an even amount of batter into each hollow and placed the tray in a 375°F preheated oven. After fifteen minutes, I retrieved them and allowed them to cool on a rack, foretasting them in my mind. When they were ready, I took one, peeled back its coat, and bit into it.

Stale-textured, mealy, and dry, like a powdery rock, my tasteless creation sucked up all the moisture in my mouth, its only redeeming quality a hint of the vanilla I had put in. It would have been more appetizing to go back to drinking the vanilla extract itself.

Dejected, I left the muffins on the counter until my dad asked me about them. I explained sheepishly that they had come out hard. And, from a man who had never baked, or so I assumed, came the single most influential lesson on baking in my life.

"Next time, don't overmix it."

III

BY THE TIME I WAS ABOUT EIGHT OR NINE YEARS OLD, I
had graduated to more complex recipes, occasionally making
desserts for dinner guests. I felt as if I had finally found something I was good at. I'd get a hot rush of pride when my mom
gloated in that self-deprecating, bored Chinese mom tone of voice,
her eyes downcast with fake disapproval, "I don't know where
she learns this, but it turns out OK. I guess I did bake a little bit a
long time ago." When translated, this meant, "My daughter is the
most talented baker in the entire universe. And by the way, she
gets it from me."

One evening a group of family friends were joining us for
dinner, so I decided to make a carrot cake. In part, I hoped to
recreate this sensation of approval.

All was going perfectly, as usual. I whisked the spices into
the flour, adding a slight warmth. I had chosen plump golden
raisins as opposed to the dark variety to stud the cake—I liked
their juicier texture and milder sweetness. As I grated the carrots
into the batter, the end slipped out of my fingers and the weight I
had placed on the hard carrot forced my knuckle into the grater,
taking off pieces of flesh along with it.

I froze, shocked. I didn't make a sound. It happened so
abruptly that it took me a few seconds to make sense of the fallen
carrot and the numbness in my knuckles. I collected myself calmly,
pulled apart the flesh of my hand to survey the damage, and took
a few minutes to treat the wound with bandages and creams.

I walked back to my cake and was flustered to find flecks of
blood on the surface of the batter where shreds of my finger had
slowly sunk in.

A panicked discussion arose inside me.

I can't serve this.

But I don't have any more carrots to make another one.

So who cares if there is no dessert tonight?

I'll just pick out what I can and finish baking it.

What if they taste it? What if they can taste finger?!

And then I remembered the sage advice from the authority of all things, Julia Child: "If you're all alone in the kitchen, nobody will know."

So I left myself in the cake, put it in the oven, baked it, iced it with cream cheese frosting, and prayed no one would discover bits of a finger. I held my breath throughout the evening, playing out every horrible scenario. And as we cut into the white frosting, and our dinner guests bit into the cake . . . I waited.

Julia was always right.

CARROT CAKE WITH CREAM CHEESE FROSTING

This recipe is written exactly as it was in the fundraising cookbook that my elementary school, Highlands Elementary School had created, except this version omits the grated finger. The recipe was contributed by Trish McMordie, and I decided not to change any of the wording, but I've included notes at the end to make it a touch tastier and a touch better, in my opinion.

I've also added a recipe for cream cheese frosting because it's so delicious with carrot cake.

⅔ cup (130 ml) vegetable oil

1 cup (250 ml) brown sugar

2 beaten eggs

1 cup (250 ml) all-purpose flour

1 teaspoon (5 ml) baking soda

1 teaspoon (5 ml) baking powder

1 teaspoon (5 ml) cinnamon

½ teaspoon (2.5 ml) salt

½ cup (125 ml) chopped nuts

1½ cups (375 ml/6 oz) grated carrots

Preheat oven to 325°F.

"Mix together oil, sugar & eggs. Sift together flour, soda, baking powder, cinnamon + salt & slowly add to the egg mixture, stirring well. Add and blend in well the nuts & carrots. Bake into a greased and floured 8"x8" pan about 30 minutes. Cool and ice with cream cheese icing."

NOTES ON THE RECIPE:

- I like to use light brown sugar as opposed to dark brown, as I find the dark has a molasses flavor that is too heavy for my taste.

- Make sure the brown sugar is packed and not loose when measuring.

- I always prefer to use fine sea salt in baking recipes.

- This recipe calls for chopped nuts, and I love toasted walnuts. Toast the walnuts in a 300°F oven for 10–15 minutes or until they are lightly toasted, being sure to toss them every 5 minutes.

- I like my carrot cakes to have warm spice flavors, so I add a ¼ teaspoon of cardamom, ¼ teaspoon of freshly grated nutmeg, $\frac{1}{8}$ teaspoon of ground cloves, and $\frac{1}{8}$ teaspoon of ground allspice to the flour mixture.

- When adding the flour mixture to the egg mixture, I stir with a wooden spoon, a mixer, or a stand mixer until it is only just combined and there are still large streaks of flour. You will be continuing to mix after you add the nuts and carrots so this keeps you from overmixing the batter, keeping the crumb tender. Then scrape the bowl well and add the nuts and carrots.

- I like raisins in my carrot cakes and added them when I was young. If you choose to, add ½ cup plump golden raisins to the batter with the nuts.

- I like to bake mine in a 9-inch round pan. Butter the inside of the pan and then line the bottom with parchment paper. To unmold, run a thin knife or offset spatula along the sides, put a plate upside down on the top of the pan and flip the entire thing so the cake is inverted onto the plate. Peel off the parchment and ice the top.

- Every oven is different. Some ovens will take up to 45–50 minutes to bake the cake. To know when it is done, take a toothpick and insert it into the center. The exact moment that the toothpick comes out clean with a few crumbs attached, the cake is done.

- You can double this recipe to make a two-layer carrot cake.

MAKES ONE 9-INCH ROUND OR 8 × 8-INCH SQUARE CAKE.

CREAM CHEESE FROSTING

1 package (8 oz) of cream cheese, room temperature

¼ cup (2 oz) unsalted butter, room temperature

1 cup (4 oz) confectioner's sugar, sifted

½ tsp fine sea salt

Seeds scraped from 1 vanilla bean

Zest of 1 lemon

Place the cream cheese and butter in a large bowl or the bowl of a stand mixer and cream them until light and airy. Slowly add the sugar and salt while mixing on low speed. Add the vanilla bean seeds and lemon zest and mix on high speed until well incorporated. Use it immediately or keep it refrigerated for up to 2 days, until you are ready to use it. If the texture is too hard, place back into the bowl of a stand mixer and mix again until the texture is spreadable.

MAKES ENOUGH FROSTING FOR A ONE-LAYER CAKE, but can be doubled for a two-layer cake.

EGGPLANT BHARTA

{2008}

I THINK THAT BY NOW I AM OLD ENOUGH,

THOUGH,

to know why SUCH THINGS HAPPEN,

OR AT LEAST HOW TO *cope with the ramifications*

AND COMPLEXITIES OF LONELINESS,

WHICH IS BY NOW MY INTIMATE AND,

I believe, MY FRIEND

M. F. K. Fisher, The Gastronomical Me,
"Sea Change"

I WAS NAÏVE, IN SOME WAYS JUST OUT OF MY MOTHER'S womb. Though twenty-six is considered to be a fully-grown adult by most standards, I still looked to others for direction and approval in the way that children do.

Perhaps it was because I was raised in a family of fiercely intelligent, headstrong, hard-nosed women—women so outspoken that there was not much space for me to fill with my thoughts or opinions before it was simply filled with theirs. It could have also been that my parents were just surviving, multitasking the heavy responsibilities of a household so full of daily needs. In reality, there was only enough to care for the family as a whole, and to take energy with temper tantrums or for my individual needs would have felt selfish, and I was probably told so. I was observant and careful not to be a burden. So from the time I began to speak, I also learned how not to.

And after some time, I forgot how to speak altogether.

I

G AND I MET WHEN WE WERE BOTH WORKING AT A LARGE design firm in Vancouver. During design college, I had become determined to gain my family's approval. Since my family gauged intelligence with academic successes, and I hadn't found many in that area, I was labeled a "lost cause" in my younger years, and I later became intensely ambitious in order to prove everyone wrong. Though my dreadful insecurity still plagued me, like so many people in their twenties, I hid behind an exaggerated display of confidence and a defiant fuchsia streak in my long black hair.

G was tall and sinewy like a jute rope, always dressed entirely in black, with dark, curly hair drooping to his shoulders and sunken eyes with hazel-colored centers that changed depending on the light or his mood. Charmingly quiet, he was self-assured and mysterious, which gave him an air of being rebellious. As we worked closely together, pushing out projects at all hours of the day and night, I found myself drawn to his confidence and unexpected sense of humor. He rarely spoke, but when he did, his surprising wit delighted me, and loud laughs jolted from my mouth before I could catch them.

We fell in love quickly. We spent hours talking, like children under the covers with a flashlight, up past our bedtime. In intimate whispers, we explored the existence of God, past lives, this life, questioned if there was more. What we didn't know just excited us. For the first time, I spoke aloud all the thoughts I had kept only for myself: I told him that I dreamt of traveling around India, that I wanted to move to another city, that I thought I was meant to do something that would help people one day—I didn't know what—that I was afraid I wasn't good enough, and G understood it all. So we decided to marry.

The night before the wedding, after months of rigorous planning, my bridesmaids, my mother, my sister, and I huddled on the floor of my parents' living room, chatting about our freshly painted nails. I quietly noted the significance of the moment to myself: I was surrounded by my closest friends and on the edge of entering a new life. Then, after the slightest pause in conversation, my mother said in a strangely casual tone, "I don't think you should marry G." She had a strained smile on her face, as if a smile would lessen the impact of her message. After another short pause, my sister admitted the same, her words hurried, as if she had been torturously holding her opinion for so long that the moment she was allowed, she ran to relieve the urge.

Silent stares filled the room. A cold sensation ran over my scalp like a rush of air, and I felt a fist-sized knot burn in my chest. I didn't have a response, so I cradled the feeling, the shock, inside of me for a moment, held it close, and felt myself curl inward for protection.

When I finally thought of what to say, I inquired with detached curiosity, "Why?"

"Because I heard you fight once . . . remember?" said my mother, trying to justify her case.

"And?" I elongated the syllable. I needed more.

"And . . . he doesn't put the toilet seat down," my sister chimed in.

Silence.

One of my bridesmaids rerouted the conversation quickly, and I waited until the mood bubbled happily again on new topics before I got up and went the bathroom, where I cried, releasing my disappointment quietly so no one would hear me. Why would they wait until the night before the wedding? What was I supposed to do now? I felt so alone without their support, and in that moment, I couldn't see my mother's concern for me; I simply felt abandoned, betrayed.

Before I left the bathroom, I dusted the remnants of tissue off my face from wiping my eyes and I surveyed myself for any signs of damage. As I stared into the mirror, the emotion drained from my reflection. In that moment I made a resolution never to include my family in my marriage. If G and I fought, I wouldn't lean on them or ask my mother or sister for advice. I vowed to speak only words of happiness, love, and respect about my husband. I would never allow my family the satisfaction of being proven right. And I would keep this moment a secret from G for our entire marriage, to protect him.

I I

THE WEDDING WAS AN EXHAUSTING 350-PERSON ORDEAL full of Chinese traditions I knew little of. I focused on our honeymoon as the light at the end of a tunnel built of toasts, handshakes, and family photographs.

Our three weeks in Greece, punctuated with a stop in Santorini, were pleasant enough. I liked the souvenirs of olive oil and oregano the most. On the second morning after we arrived, we woke in the bright, whitewashed hotel room surrounded by the bluest sea. I was indulging in the luxury of rest, glad to be rid of weddings and errands, stretching off sleep with a playful fancy to stay in bed and sprawl like a cat for a moment longer. I don't remember who suggested we start our day of exploring, but I said in a light and lazy sort of way, "Why don't you hop in the shower first and I'll follow you?"

"Why should I? Why don't you shower first?" he asked, his tone abrupt and cool.

"Well I didn't think it was a big deal, I just wanted a moment," I explained.

"Well if it's not a big deal, then why don't you go ahead?"

I was so shocked by the faint breath of bitterness coming from him. I had never seen him so offended before. Shocked and unsure of what to do next, I turned over to read a book, pretending not to notice much. I half-expected us to laugh at how ludicrous the situation was, but this inexplicable encounter transformed itself into a silent feud.

We sat there, silently, for so many hours that when what was once the morning sun began to set, I finally gave in. I got up and went to the bathroom to shower.

As I stood under the shower, I began to hit myself repeatedly on the face, the sound and my cries muffled by the hot, streaming water. It came out of nowhere like an instinct, to hit myself, and I did it out of an intense confusion, not knowing what to make of G's cold reaction. It came from frustration for not knowing what to say, for feeling cornered for reasons I didn't even understand. I detested myself because I felt mute, as if I had betrayed myself, abandoned without words to explain it all.

III

DESPITE BEING RAISED BY SO MANY DOMINANT WOMEN, I was somehow firmly invested in a husband's right to guide the direction of a family and the wife's duty to follow. I had absorbed the idea that married women were to act modest and wholesome, that they should be careful with speech and dress for some doctrinal reason. Wild words like "fuck" and "shit" were to be avoided.

Of all the quirky things I assumed about marriage, I'm very grateful I believed this particular myth: that all wives cooked and baked. When G and I returned home from our honeymoon, I dusted off my kitchen skills for the first time in a decade and reacquainted myself with an old love.

We took turns cooking. G was extremely fair, dividing everything down the middle with the accuracy of a mathematician. At times this was done superbly, but other times he forgot to—and realistically no one could entirely—account for all the variables of life when putting them on a scale. How could one accurately measure things like joy or passion and what it is worth to another to experience them? And it's difficult to compare the value of a gift when it holds more than can be counted. But when it came to chores, we decided that he would cook one week, I would wash dishes, and then we would trade.

We cooked every night, allowing ourselves an inexpensive meal at a restaurant once a week and fine restaurants four times a year, on our birthdays, our anniversary, and on Valentine's Day, as a way to stick to a strict budget. We were saving for the future—maybe kids or a house, for everything and anything.

But as our marriage progressed, the budget began to feel more and more constricting to me, though I didn't fully stop to understand and acknowledge it. We rarely traveled at all, taking mostly just local weekend trips every now and then. And although I had been promoted quickly and made a very healthy salary, I had a monthly spending allowance of $225, which was to cover everything deemed "extraneous," like coffee, clothing, makeup, glasses, books and magazines, hobbies, going out with friends, and entertainment that we didn't do together as a couple.

So, in addition to our budget, G both implied and vocalized thoughts on life, behavior, dress. And since I hadn't truly learned to wonder what I thought, I had a void where my opinions should be, and I looked to my husband to fill it. I took his word for all of it. The more I forced him to lend me his opinions, the less I trusted myself to know my own. Though his decidedness to my uncertainty was likely what attracted me to him in the first place, that role in our marriage began to feel suffocating.

G was private. He kept mostly to himself, had just a few friends that he spoke to on occasion, and rarely went out. He insisted that we not answer phone calls from unknown telephone numbers or open the door to friends unexpectedly dropping by to say hello. I believe it was to protect our privacy, but over time, I longed to invite friends over for dinner, on weekends for coffee, and especially over the holidays. Entertaining had been such a large part of my childhood, but G felt that it was an invasion of his personal space. I didn't disagree, and I didn't see how I could.

Then, little by little, I disagreed even less. I stopped trying to suggest artwork to fill our blank walls, or that we should buy bedside tables for the bedroom, or a paper towel holder, or a new kettle, because G wanted every decision to be jointly made, and it was exhausting. It was rare that I could spend money on things that he found illogical, like a glass of wine, coffee, or travel, because I couldn't justify them in his mind. I was never allowed to spend money independently, outside of my allowance, because decisions to spend $10 or $1,000 needed to be jointly made, too, and I was never good at debates. So I gave up, and the more I conceded, the more I felt as if I was living in a room being filled with G's boxes, making it harder for me to find space to breathe.

But food, lucky for me, was a necessity. We had to eat, and we had to cook because we rarely ate out. And because we took turns cooking, we didn't have to decide together, and G didn't have to agree and didn't get the chance to disagree either. I was free to cook what I liked, try something new, make decisions, buy ingredients. I found space in the kitchen to be free, and I abused it exhaustively as a way to express my creativity and independence, and as a means to exercise my need to explore. I made French cakes that took days to create. I tried complex dishes I'd never tasted before but was so curious about, like mole sauces and handmade tamales with only a recipe, Googled pictures, and Wikipedia descriptions. I submerged myself in food as a way to be distracted from all the feelings I couldn't yet make sense of. It was not only a safe hiding place and a playground, but when the cakes came out moist and the sauces ethereal, I was proud of myself and slowly felt that maybe I was capable.

One night when I was alone at home, I stumbled on a recipe for eggplant bharta, a dish that I had never tried. Maybe it was the description of it that I found alluring ("Indian-spiced mash smoothed with a swirl of yogurt"), or the fact that eggplant was one of my favorite vegetables (passive, with a notable ability to hold every good flavor within it). It looked comforting, exotic, and on inspection of my cupboards, I realized I had all of the major ingredients. So I began cooking, taking time, feeling the knife under my palm, running my fingers along the shiny black skin of the eggplant, and toasting the spices slowly until a fragrant gust rose up to me. I added the onions and caramelized them until they were dry and sweet, stopping to taste at every step and feeling the warm sensation of ginger or the tang of tomato on my tongue. I simmered the curry for as long as it took for the disparate elements to fold into one another, surrendering their own individualities to a greater good.

And when it was ready, I ate each bite with a fluffy mound of basmati rice, closing my eyes alone at the dinner table, feeling the delightful pop of each little green pea in my mouth every now and again.

I V

THE AUTUMN BEFORE THE BAKERY OPENED, G MOVED out. The night before and the day of his move, I stayed with a friend, away from our apartment. It was a way to survive. I couldn't watch it. The morning G left, my friend and I went for a croissant at a pâtisserie, sat at a round bistro table, and slowly sipped coffees and chatted as if nothing was out of the ordinary. And after enough time had passed, after I was sure that G was gone, I returned home.

I hesitantly opened the door to the home I had shared with my husband for the last eight years. When I walked in, I found that he had moved out. There was almost nothing left: no couch, no bed, only the dust that collected around the spots where the furniture had been, delineating the emptiness. He had taken exactly what we had agreed upon one night at the dining room table, but the place seemed emptier than I envisioned. My home was no longer a home. It was hollow.

I paused for a moment, imperceptible to anyone but me, and then immediately jumped into action, walking straight into the apartment, the center of the pain, exposing myself and hoping the repeated exposure would dull it enough for me to come out the other side better in some way. I forced myself to vacuum, and then I created a makeshift sofa out of an old futon, a bedsheet, and some pillows. Since G and I had been sleeping in different bedrooms, with me in the smaller of the two, I moved my bedroom furniture back into the larger room.

Over the next few days, I did all the things I'd wanted to do for the last eight years: I painted the walls a sleepy rose color, and I went out and bought a paper towel holder.

When I had changed the apartment to an arbitrary "enough," I collapsed on my bed, drained of every ounce of will, and I called my mom.

"Hello?"

"It's me, Jackie."

"What's wrong?"

"He's gone," I said so quietly she couldn't hear me.

"What?"

"He's GONE."

And I sobbed, mournful sounds that no one had heard since I knew how to be ashamed, wails coming from beneath the pain and loss. And my mother just cried with me, knowing to love me in that way, in that moment.

EGGPLANT BHARTA

I know this recipe is far from traditional, but I don't think the original was meant to be either. I have also evolved this recipe from the one I originally made, because I, too, have evolved and so it should be.

3 large eggplants (about 3½ lb total)

¼ cup mustard oil (or substitute vegetable oil)

1 tsp whole cumin seeds

2 tsp coriander seeds, crushed

½ tsp whole mustard seeds

2 medium yellow onions, finely chopped

2 tsp salt, divided

1 green chili or small jalapeño, seeded and finely chopped

4 garlic cloves, minced

2 tbsp grated fresh ginger

2 tbsp tomato paste

1 tsp red Kashmiri chili powder

4 ripe medium tomatoes, finely chopped

1 tsp turmeric

1 tsp garam masala

1 cup fresh or frozen peas

¾ cup chopped cilantro

⅓–½ cup whole milk or plain yogurt

Garam masala, for serving

Preheat the oven to 500°F.

Place the shiny eggplants on a baking sheet lined with aluminum foil. Pierce the smooth skins all over with a sharp paring knife or fork. Bake them in the oven for about 45 minutes to 1 hour or until the skins are scorched and crumpled, the bodies are sagging, and the flesh feels very soft when pressed lightly. Set them aside to cool until you can handle them with your fingers.

Peel the crisped skin off the flesh, and collect the flesh into a large bowl, scraping it off with a large spoon if it sticks to the skins. Mash the flesh coarsely with a fork and set aside.

Warm the oil over medium-high heat in a large pan. Sprinkle in the cumin, coriander, and mustard seeds and cook until they begin to sizzle, become fragrant, and pop, about 10 seconds. Turn the heat down to medium for more gentle cooking and stir in the onion and ½ teaspoon of salt, and cook until the onion is soft and translucent but not browned, 5–10 minutes.

Add the chopped green chili, garlic, ginger, tomato paste, and chili powder and cook, stirring slowly and constantly. A spicy aroma will rise from the pot. Continue cooking for about 2 minutes, careful to just warm the spices without allowing them to burn.

Scatter the fresh tomatoes and another ½ teaspoon of salt into the pan, and stir, scraping the spices off the bottom of the pan to incorporate. Simmer for about 10 minutes, until most of the liquid has evaporated, the sauce thickens, and your entire kitchen is scented with spice. Add the turmeric and garam masala and stir for another 2–3 minutes until the spices meld into the dish.

Place the eggplant into the sauce, stir to combine, and cook over low heat for 15–25 minutes until the separate elements begin to look like one dish and most of the liquid has evaporated into a thick sauce. This is when you want to be patient and continue cooking it until you are sure it has all come together. It shouldn't seem like many ingredients in a pot, but rather a smooth, silky curry. Taste as you go; it's the only way to be sure.

Fold in the peas, and cook to warm through. Reduce the heat to low, and stir in the cilantro, yogurt, and remaining 1 teaspoon of salt.

Serve hot, or better yet, just warmed, sprinkled with a pinch of garam masala and alongside a bed of fluffy basmati rice, steamed with a few whole cardamom pods and some chopped onions. Eat, taking time to taste and savor each bite.

A NOTE ON THE MEASUREMENTS: I have left this recipe in volume measurements, as it is meant to be a recipe for home. However, I suggest tasting it along the way and using your instincts. You'll know if it tastes great to you. It's such a nice experience to cook with a recipe for inspiration and not a rule.

MAKES 4–6 SERVINGS.

THE TWIN

{2010}

WHEN SHALL WE LIVE *if not* NOW?

M. F. K. Fisher, Serve It Forth, *"Meals for Me"*

THERE ARE MOMENTS IN LIFE THAT WE MAY, AT TIMES, regret. We think of them as mistakes, still feeling their pangs, before we gently remind ourselves that the circumstances, actions, words spoken, and the choices we make are mere stones that pave the road we explore, perfect in its own way. And the more of the road we see, the less we tend to regret.

I

"I WANT TO GO TO ART SCHOOL . . . IN TORONTO," I declared to my mother, despite my family's dissatisfaction. They were convinced that I would inevitably starve in exactly the same fashion as many artists had done before me, only to be redeemed in death.

Going to art school wasn't a decision I took lightly. For most children of Asian families, university science programs were the only acceptable path: it was the most difficult to achieve and showed the greatest financial promise. Almost all other paths were seen as embarrassing and shameful "plan B"s. Though I knew my decision would disappoint the family, I didn't really see a choice; I simply didn't believe I was good at anything else. My parents seemed to hold back their praise and encouragement of my artistic abilities, fearful I would follow that career path, but I received awards and recognition throughout school, so I was just relieved that I was good at *something*. I was good at art, and I hung onto that as one of the few things that made me special, even though I knew it wasn't much to my family.

So I went into the high school guidance counselor's office at lunchtime one afternoon and stared at a wall of university and college brochures. I picked up an application for an art school in Toronto—somewhere far away and big—and one for a local school as a backup in case I didn't get in.

In my parents' eyes, I was stubborn and tenacious about certain things. I rarely allowed anyone to change my mind after I had decided what I truly wanted, and I think my mother knew this. "Sure. If you get straight A's and early acceptance into a university science program, I'll let you go to art school," she replied simply. I understood it as a fair compromise and began the year of studying, drawing, painting, and planning at all hours of the day and night, focused only on my goal.

My mind was never one for memorizing dates, names, and disjointed facts. Knowing this, I studied for my exams for twice as long as other students, reading and rereading textbook chapters, burning the image of each page into my mind until I could visualize every word and color. Often I would study until it was time to go to school again in the morning, and on other evenings, I attended portfolio-building classes at a local college to make sure I had the requirements needed to impress the art colleges. My more academic family members and classmates would often tease me, amused at how much of an effort I was making because it came easily to them and they didn't understand.

After semesters of math tutors, study groups, and befriending library regulars on my lunch breaks to discuss chemistry problems, I succeeded: I managed to get near perfect grades, early acceptance to a science program at a university in Vancouver, as well as to art school in Toronto.

My mother was stunned. It was late in the evening, and she was getting ready for bed, but she stopped and looked at me, searching my eyes with a look of confusion on her face. She thought to herself, perhaps not meaning to say it aloud to me, "I only said yes because I didn't think you could do it."

Those words. How sad, angry, insulted I felt, and yet how proud as well. My mother didn't mean it to be hurtful; in fact, I think she was impressed. That evening I learned that there was a chance my future was not as hopeless as I had believed. I had been taunted and told as a child that all the brains must have gone to other members of the family. Family would tell me that I was not really deserving of our family name because I was obviously not as smart as they were. And my aunts and mom were sure that I would have to marry rich because I wasn't smart enough to be successful on my own. I was terrified that it was true and also determined to work as hard as I could to prove everyone wrong. I never wanted to be labeled as stupid or useless again.

I I

AS PLANNED, I MOVED TO TORONTO FOR ART SCHOOL, and it wasn't long before my partially baked, sensational plans of being a famous photojournalist for *National Geographic* and publishing a coffee table book, all by the age of twenty-five, were slightly derailed. After I began my photography studies, I became disheartened by what I observed within this new art community.

Professors seemed to skip over the fundamentals of art, glossing over skills and techniques to push modern conceptual art, and students were graded on how provocative their work was.

Students who procrastinated on six-month projects learned a popular trick to coming up with something to hand in: all they needed was nudity and a little bullshit. It was quite simple: cast your penis in bronze and talk about our culture's antiquated ideologies of male stereotypes. Create a childlike painting with your pubic hair—must still be attached to the labia for true effect—and talk about the discordant messages on youth and sexuality from media and pop culture. (And we all knew the artist painted in a juvenile style, not for conceptual commentary on society but because neither she nor her labia were very deft at painting to begin with.) I watched this happen over and over again, and then began to question whether I was learning anything of true value in art school. But I couldn't admit to my family that they might have been right about my career path, that it was a waste of time and I would end up jobless and starving. So I kept going, but I abandoned any clear path toward being a photographer. Instead, I took random courses in topics that I was interested in, such as jewelry-making and electronic installation art, where we spent an entire semester soldering electronic components for motion-activated lights while talking about the Clinton administration and books by Gabriel García Márquez. I took paper-making, Chinese painting, figure drawing, and film classes, just aimless and wandering in the world of art.

By the time I was in my early twenties, I found myself with a lot of random skills, none of which were employable in itself. I could draw, bind books, make rings, make artisan paper from strands of sisal, use medium- and large-format cameras, talk at length about the history of Japanese film, have intellectual art critiques, and communicate with someone with nothing but a canvas and paint. So I painted, selling canvases when I could, and worked odd jobs: an illustrator for a men's fashion designer, a salesperson at a gallery on the east side of Toronto that sold African masks. I was surviving as many artists had done before and around me, confused about what I should do next.

"Should I go back to school to get an official degree? Should I learn something else? Should I just be an artist forever? Should I . . ." I asked my good friend S for the hundredth time over a bowl of cheap noodles in Koreatown.

She listened patiently to the same conversation we'd been having for months, and finally, as if the moment was ripe (or perhaps her impatience was), she said, "Jackie, it is hard to know what is down the road if you've never been there. I think perhaps you should just take a step and start to walk." S was naïve about everything except the wisest topics. She was from a wealthy family in India, and while I often got the sense that she could barely tie her own shoes, she'd sometimes surprise me with her insights on life.

So after a year of trying to make it work in Toronto, I reluctantly went back to Vancouver, with no credentials to my name. I immediately missed my independent life out East, but I took my friend's advice and started walking in any direction: working as a nanny disguised as an art teacher and applying to interior and graphic design programs that seemed to have good earning potential; waiting for life to reveal itself to me. I wasn't particularly passionate or even sure of any one career direction, but I wanted to get my life started as soon as possible. I eventually settled on going back to school for graphic design and illustration, because I was allowed to skip the first year of the program based on my past education.

When I walked into a classroom on the first day, everyone looked up at me: thirty students in front of their computers, their desks decorated with photos, past projects, and inside jokes. I was scared, worried that I wouldn't be able to catch up. I sat at the empty desk in the middle of the room, and after I settled in, a girl with a platinum blonde bob leaned over. "Hey, I'm T. Are you nervous?"

I sat up taller and looked at her over my shoulder. "Why should I be?" I reasoned to myself that acting confident was better than showing how unsure I was.

"I don't know. All these new people?"

"Well, they're either going to like me or not. There's not much I can do about it."

"Well, that's good," she said hesitantly, startled by my brusque response. In all honesty, I did care if they liked me, but I had also decided that I was there to succeed and make something of myself. Even if it meant being disliked, I needed to focus on being the best.

After a few weeks of classes, I was delighted to discover I had a passion and talent for the topics we were learning—typography, illustration, visual communication and storytelling, conceptual development. I discovered that I innately knew how to tinker with aesthetics, to combine shapes, colors, textures, words, and volumes of visual cues to communicate complex concepts. I understood the subtleties of the visual language and of communication. I was good at it, and I remembered again what it was like to be good at something.

"It's like the teachers love everything you do!" a classmate said to me one afternoon on our lunch break.

"What do you mean?"

"Everything you did to my project, the professors loved. How do you know?" she exclaimed, mystified. I had just helped her with a project that was failing miserably.

I didn't know. I hadn't thought about it before. It all just felt quite natural. I thought of my family, how I spent years as a quiet child, afraid of being a burden to my family. I watched intently and learned a language that was never spoken. So much was communicated with a furrowed brow, a sarcastic tone of voice, or the way we dressed for an occasion. When my mom wore makeup, I knew I would have to be extra well-behaved that evening. If she wore red, it was probably a traditional event, and if she wore an expensive dress with a brand name, it was because she wanted to impress someone. My mom would unconsciously mumble to herself the things she felt while driving or cooking by herself, thinking that no one was listening. But I would listen carefully, and I developed a kind of Rosetta Stone for deciphering her language. As I learned to read the layers beneath my mother's communication, I gained an intuitive sense of what people wanted but never said. But I didn't know how to explain this to my friend in words, so I just shrugged and replied, smiling, "I don't know!"

III

I HAD THE HIGH-PAYING JOB, THE CONDO, I WAS MAKING my yearly retirement plan contributions, I was married: all the boxes for "success" seemed to be checked. But now that I was surrounded with everything I had been told I was supposed to want, the veneer began to crack.

I was exhausted from the long hours and stress of trying to get ahead in my work. I was at the office past midnight and every weekend. I took on so many projects that I did the work of three people. The office simply didn't know how to deal with the number of overtime hours I accumulated. When the pressure to be creative, successful, and worthy mixed with looming deadlines and self-doubt, I would take five-minute breaks to cry in the bathroom until I felt ready to tackle the next task. And even though I was achieving my goals, being promoted from entry-level designer to account manager, senior designer, essentially acting as the art director in three and a half years, I began to feel despondent and disconnected without really knowing why. And as more time passed, the veneer buckled further.

Desperate for a change, G and I left the firm and started our own. It was lucrative, and the work was steady and secure, but a few years into it, things inevitably began feeling routine again. I needed a challenge, a distraction.

"G, maybe we could do more. We could take on more projects, different ones and hire freelancers. What do you think?" I asked him one day in our home office.

"I like the way things are. If we expand, then our lives will change; it'll get more complicated. I don't know if I want that," G said. So we stayed exactly the same, day after day, while a yearning for something I hadn't seen yet bubbled on the back burner, getting more concentrated year after year.

I V

ONCE, WHEN I WAS A CHILD, WE FOUND LITTLE WHITISH worms in our big bag of rice. There they were, barely noticeable except for the dark ridges across their bellies that we could see if we looked closely enough. Being a young family, and having so many mouths to feed, it was more of a loss than anyone in the family said out loud. I watched my mother begin to separate the bugs out, grain by grain, until my dad, standing beside her, said, "It's not worth your effort. Just throw it out." It was true. It didn't matter how the bugs got to be there; it wasn't something we could have avoided. It just was, and regardless of how hard she might try to fix it, the rice couldn't be eaten anymore.

V

"G, I THINK I'M READY TO HAVE KIDS. I'D LIKE TO TALK about it with you but want to give you time to prepare and think. Shall we set a time to talk in a month?"

This was the way we interacted. I spoke to G very prudently, even formally, a reflection of the many rules and boundaries that had been created between us over time. As I spoke today, I made sure to be even more careful. This was important. I needed him to be receptive, so I chose my words precisely and practiced them in my mind a few times before I said them aloud.

On our second date, I had said to G, "I have always wanted to be a mother, to have two or three children. It's what I feel like I'm meant to do, and I can't imagine a life without being a mother. So if you don't want the same thing, there's no point in dating me." He smiled and nervously admitted that he wanted the same. After we decided to marry, we planned to wait for a few years to give ourselves time to settle into married life.

In our first year of marriage I had found a box of vintage wooden blocks with the alphabet carved into the faces alongside pictograms for each letter—an apple for A, a bumble bee for B. I wrapped this box of blocks in green holiday paper with a gold bow before our first Christmas together and placed it under the tree every Christmas, for our future baby.

Four years passed. When one of my best friends had her first child, I flew to Toronto to help. I did laundry, cooked, burped, and bounced the newborn baby so my friend could recover. One day when I was changing the baby's diaper, his clear eyes connected to mine. He smiled wide and laughed gently, and I was sure he knew me. I knew I loved him very much. That was the moment I was sure I was ready to be a mom. So I chose the right moment to bring up the subject again with G.

"I'm not sure I want to have kids anymore," he replied.

"Why?" I asked, stoically. I knew the reason was unimportant. I knew his mind was made up, and I was not going to change it. But because he wanted six months to think about it, I waited.

For those six months, I imagined life without children, something I had never done before. What would I do with my time? What was the purpose of my life? I questioned why I had let becoming a mother define so much of my future self. Would I be happy without children? Would I be sad? Lonely? Would the regret become so overwhelming that I would come to resent G later? My mind paced back and forth. The wait felt like the hours I spent in the hospital, waiting for the doctor's diagnosis on my grandmother's impending death. All this time I was full of dread, patiently, fearing for the life of a child that didn't yet exist. And in the end, G's decision didn't change.

I agonized over what to do next for months. I sat with my friend B for hours, wondering aloud about everything worrying me. Could I have children with someone else? Could I leave G? If I was going to resent him anyway, perhaps it would be best to leave now. But was it fair to compare my future husband to G? It was true that things were not perfect with G, I wasn't always happy, but we had perfect moments, too . . . And he was my husband and I depended on him. I would feel lost without him. He was the only thing I knew when I didn't know myself. But although he was my whole world, children were the only future I had imagined for us.

I weighed my options, back and forth, based on how heavy the regret might feel on my shoulders. I couldn't blame G for changing his mind. I understood that people did.

One night, I asked him to sit with me on the couch. I explained that if I left him, there was a chance I would regret it. And knowing that children absorb subtle emotions, I foresaw the possibility that my child would feel my sacrifice and become sad or resentful toward me in return. I didn't want that under any circumstance. So I chose G, and I promised myself never to resent him for the decision I made to stay, without children.

VI

BEFORE I LEFT FOR PARIS, THERE WAS A PERIOD IN MY life when planning "who was bringing the potato salad" to a potluck was a much more frequent topic of conversation than it was after. From the time I was born right up to the decision not to have children, I had prepared for the practicalities of having a family by watching new mothers and learning from them. I quietly collected information about the best strollers and the most effective anti-stretch mark creams. I didn't plan to quit my work; I wanted to keep my career and juggle both, as my mother had.

When most of my friends were swirling in storms of diapers, temper tantrums, play dates, and backyard barbecues, I had been right there with them, secretly planning which cookies to pack in my children's lunches so they had the most bargaining power on the playground. Then when my life shifted in a childless direction, there was an empty space amid everything else that had remained unchanged. Day-to-day life went on as usual, but the soundless space beside what had filled it before was like the tiny pause after a heartbeat.

G and I drove out to a party at a friend's house in a suburb just like the one I had planned to settle down in with my husband

and children. I brought with me a large platter of homemade cookies and bars and was greeted by a friendly group of newly-weds and newly adults. We stood in the kitchen of a townhouse in a sprawling network of townhouses, each with their own white garage and little square patch of garden. I began chatting with a man in his mid-twenties with dark hair and an accent shared by his twin brother, with virtually the same clear eyes but a more sedate demeanor.

After telling him I was a designer, I asked him about himself. He beamed and explained that he was days away from moving to Montreal to be with a woman he barely knew, but loved instantly. I was enraptured by the monologue he had been waiting to unload, and as his willing recipient, listened as he went on to detail his plan to buy a charming vineyard in the countryside of Spain and begin his life as a winemaker.

I ate every delicious morsel of his life, filling in the parts he left open with my own dreamy details. Obviously the vineyard had a farmhouse that could be renovated, and though it would be cold in the winters, there were large seventeenth-century hearths to keep warm by and cozy quilts found at local markets. My imagination followed him so deep into this fantasy, that I could see the rows of vines outside of the kitchen window and feel the dog pawing for scraps at my feet.

It was so utopian—the kind of story that you'd only see in movies or read in books. The kind of life that "other people" have, not someone I could know and certainly not me . . . but here was one of those people, standing in front of me. I was in awe of what he planned to accomplish, and of the bravery it took.

When I relayed his story to our friends afterward, excited, they rolled their eyes, looking back and forth at each other and shaking their heads.

"Oh, you mean E . . . Yeah, he's a character all right. It's different every month with him. He falls in love with someone new, picks up, moves, and just starts doing the exact same work. One month he's in love with a naturopath in Calgary, the next a cheese maker in the Okanagan, and next is Montreal."

Perhaps it was too good to be true after all. Even still, there was something in E's story that lingered on my mind. There was a fearlessness, a thirst that I caught that was so familiar to me. My subconscious recognized a hidden part of me, and thousands of thoughts began to rush into my mind. "So what if E is flaky and impulsive? I'm not. I don't have to go the extreme of following naturopaths around the country. I know how to be practical; I've been practical for a long time! Why can't I travel, live in a different country, or indulge myself in a passion, too?" Maybe there were more ways to live life beyond buying a home, having kids, and discussing potato salads.

On the car ride home, I started thinking aloud to G.

"What are we working for? What are we doing with our lives? What is this all for if we don't live? Why don't we just take a year and live in Europe? Buy a vineyard? Or travel? Or do something . . . anything else?" Since he allowed me to carry on for so long, I knew he was curious, too.

And then I took out the one weapon I had at my disposal. "I mean, if I have to live without children, I want all the benefits of it, too. All the money we would have spent on kids, I want to spend on us. I want to travel, I want to do all the things that people with kids can't do."

G finally spoke. "OK, let's think about this. Let's take six months and think about whether this is something we really want to do, and what we would do if we did."

That was more than enough for me, and it was the only time I brought up the topic of children again.

VII

I THOUGHT ABOUT LIFE AND WHAT I WANTED OUT OF IT. I broke down everything I assumed my life was supposed to be, examined each part, and redefined it all, one block at a time. I asked myself what I truly valued. I asked myself what I wanted my legacy to be, what kind of person I would be proud to say I was, what I would be proud to say I accomplished. I considered what I would be willing to sacrifice and what I had been told was important but in the end really wasn't.

For months, I wrote enormous lists of things I loved, wanted, didn't want, and couldn't live without, and began whittling it down. In the end, there was just one item.

On my deathbed, it would fill me with joy to know that I was brave enough to live life's greatest potential. The only thing I would regret would be not having done that.

POTATO SALAD

After I began travel writing, I went to one of the most magical places in Northern British Columbia, a place called Bella Coola. We saw savage and untouched wilderness with hardy wildflowers growing between mammoth granite slabs when we went heli-hiking in the mountains, and we boated in sage-colored glacial waters to hidden hot springs along the rocky shores. When I came home, I created this potato salad, inspired by the whole roasted salmon dinners and potato salads made with new potatoes just plucked from the earth that morning.

FOR THE PICKLED SHALLOTS
1 tbsp (15 ml) sugar
¼ cup (60 ml) white wine vinegar
2 tbsp (30 ml) water
1 medium shallot, thinly sliced in rounds

Place the thinly sliced shallots in a medium heat-proof bowl. In a small pot, bring the sugar, vinegar, and water to a boil. Allow the sugar to dissolve. Pour the hot liquid on the shallots and let rest at room temperature for at least 1 hour. Can be made ahead and kept refrigerated for a week.

FOR THE ROASTED POTATOES
2 lb (900 g) small red-skinned potatoes, halved or quartered
4 cloves garlic, peeled
3 tbsp (45 ml) olive oil
¾ tsp (3.75 ml) sea salt
½ tsp (2.5 ml) pepper
2 large sprigs of thyme
5–6 strips of lemon peel

Preheat the oven to 450°F.

Mix all of the ingredients on a sheet tray lined with parchment paper. Place in the oven and roast for about 30 minutes or until the potatoes are soft when pierced with a knife, and golden and caramelized on the edges. Remove and discard the lemon peel and thyme after roasting, as these were only for aromatic purposes.

FOR THE AIOLI

1 clove garlic, finely grated

½ tsp (2.5 ml) sea salt

¼ tsp (1.25 ml) pepper

1 egg yolk

½ tsp (2.5 ml) Dijon mustard

Juice and zest of 1 lemon

¼ cup (60 ml) olive oil

In a medium bowl, whisk together all of the ingredients except the oil. Slowly add the oil in a thin stream while whisking, and continue to whisk until the mixture begins to thicken and lighten. The dressing should not be entirely emulsified; it should still be thin enough to drizzle. Can be made up to 2 hours ahead of time and kept refrigerated.

TO ASSEMBLE THE SALAD

½ cup (125 ml) smoky candied salmon, broken into small chunks

⅓ cup (75 ml) Italian parsley leaves

⅓ cup (75 ml) celery leaves

1 celery stalk, cut into a small dice

6 radishes, sliced thinly

Place potatoes on a plate or in a bowl. Top with the pickled shallots, candied salmon, parsley, celery leaves, celery, and radishes. Drizzle aioli on the salad right before serving and mix if desired.

A NOTE ON MEASUREMENTS: I've left this recipe mostly in volume measurements as this is a recipe for home, and it is flexible enough that the measurements do not need to be so precise.

SERVES 4–6 AS A SIDE DISH OR 6–8 AT A POTLUCK.

FARMERS' MARKET, VANCOUVER

{2008}

I STILL THINK THAT ONE OF THE

PLEASANTEST OF ALL EMOTIONS IS TO KNOW

that I, I with my brain and my hands, have nourished

THERE'S SOMETHING THAT HAPPENS IN A PERSON WHEN hunger and hope are fused together. I think "obsessed" would be the appropriate word. And that I was.

For others it could have been dancing, world history, maybe even model airplanes, but it was food that I fixated on. I needed it. Not in the way we all need it, as sustenance, but as a life raft in the middle of an ocean of depression with nothing else surrounding me except empty water and the empty sky above it. I clung to it because it was the only hope that I might find shore.

Depressed, I existed in a thick shadow where everything was deadened. I was perpetually trapped in that one moment during winter when the sun has just set and everything seems that much more lifeless. Most of the time, I couldn't feel, and when I could, *my beloved few, that I have concocted a stew or a story,*

a rarity or a plain dish,

TO SUSTAIN THEM TRULY AGAINST

THE HUNGERS OF THE WORLD.

M. F. K. Fisher, The Gastronomical Me,
"The Measure of My Powers"

it hurt and I hated it more. But occasionally I caught the scent of a roasting chicken or a bush of bristly rosemary in a garden warmed from the sun, and I would drift along with it for a delicious moment.

The scent of fresh basil or ripe tomatoes and the grassy vines they clung to, seeing bright yellow zucchini with wilted white petals hanging from their ends, the feel of soft fennel fronds like peacock feathers, the smell of garlicky sauces reducing or hot chorizo sautéed with onions—these all made my body respond. I felt something and I wanted to feel it again.

Touch, memory, and spice—these all began to revive me at a cellular level. Each dish I cooked was another stroke of the paddle, and in time I spotted a speck on the horizon that spurred me to paddle faster and harder. And as I paddled farther, what was once a tiny speck became the outline of a city. With every course, I floated closer to the living.

I

MARKETS FLOODED ME WITH LIFE. THEIR COLORFUL produce, the growth in each season on display, vendors selling flowers relaxed in full bloom, little pots of demi-glace, imported cheeses, and pecan shortbread that melted in my mouth. Around Easter, the local charcuterie would post fluorescent reminders to preorder hams, and I fantasized about baking them with honey and grainy mustard or brushing the top with a sticky, sweet pineapple-soy glaze, allowing the crust to caramelize and crystallize into a meaty lacquer box.

I would walk past each brightly colored stall, dawdling under the pretense of "grocery shopping" but secretly playing hooky from work, concocting imaginary meals with cans of smoky peppers in adobo sauce, white onions, cilantro, and masa flour, or sniffing varieties of Italian oregano like little green pearls still on their stems, or bright green olive oils, and tasting the slow progression of a tomato sauce in my mind.

I watched old movies about food, like *Big Night* and *Mostly Martha*, while I scoured blogs and websites in different languages for obscure recipes. I took on one recipe and then the next, madly working my way through countless books. My shelves were full of *Gourmet, Bon Appétit*, Martha Stewart, Maida Heatter, Rose Levy Beranbaum, Julia Child, Pierre Hermé, Dorie Greenspan, and Patricia Wells. I took books out from the library like when I was a child. I cooked from Deborah Madison's vegetarian tome, got an Italian education from Marcella Hazan, and read books on canning, making jam, and growing food, poring over everything I could about those topics. I carried in my purse books by Michael Pollan and Margaret Visser, biographies on Jacques Pépin, and *The Taste of Country Cooking* by Edna Lewis. But most importantly, it was M. F. K. Fisher who fed me stories that made me laugh, dream, wonder, and remember again what it felt like to be alive.

I searched for the perfect everything, from pound cakes to roasts, sour cherries to pork bellies. I was insatiable, and when I had consumed every bit of information that books and the internet could provide, I saved for weekend courses at local cooking schools. With textbooks in hand, I was both challenged and lulled to sleep as I read, cradling their weight in my lap before bedtime.

In the quiet church of my own kitchen, I cooked with the intensity of prayer as G looked on, uninterested. He didn't care much about food, but that didn't stop me. And when I shared what my hands had made, I saw that my friends and family tasted joy in my pies and passion in the glazes on my cakes. Although their hungers were different than mine, I understood them all the same and it gave me much pleasure to satisfy them, too.

I knew, though, that they didn't fully understand how urgently I was tied to food, and I was always aware of that strange separation. It was faint, and if you didn't know it was there, you might not think to ask. But I noticed it when I spoke of chocolate and the fine nuances in it: fruity, smoky, red or green. They could taste the flavors, but we did not taste the same thing. I would look longingly into their faces, searching their expressions and hoping to recognize myself in them, but I never did. I accepted that I never would, but I wasn't sad; it was enough for me just to know I'd had a hand in feeding them in any way at all.

11

"I'M NOT SURE YOU SHOULD BE BAKING ANYMORE," G SAID
to me one evening.

"What? Why?" I shook my head in shock and disbelief. I thought I had misheard.

"It's just expensive. We can't eat it all, and you're just giving it all away." It was true. I was giving away layer cakes, muffins, cookies, and biscotti to anyone who would still agree to take them, their waistlines growing with my curiosity.

But how could I go about giving up something that was my life raft, something so much a part of me? My best friend, B, looked at me with concern in her glacial blue eyes. "But it makes you so happy. How could you stop?" I didn't know either.

I tumbled the dilemma around in my mind for weeks. I needed to find a solution. If it was the cost that G was uncomfortable with, then it shouldn't be a problem if I paid for it. But how would I find the money? My personal budget wouldn't allow it. If I could find a way to sell the pastries, it would pay for my exploration . . . Then I had it: I could start a home bakery, selling at farmers' markets. G couldn't disagree, so I began, knowing I didn't know where to begin.

I Googled everything, from "how to start a home-based bakery" to "how to sell at farmers' markets." I called markets for information on how to apply, which led me to city requirements on running a food-based business. I took a step wherever I saw one: a food-safe class, creating menus around what I was allowed to sell according to the government health board, applying at smaller markets on the outskirts of the city to gain more credibility so I could be considered for the larger markets within the city.

G agreed to lend me $2,000 from our personal accounts to

buy the required tents, plates, and equipment, and eventually, it seemed I had a little business. I named it Yummy Baked Goods. I designed my logo and business cards, and I made cookies and squares and cakes. I felt as if I was awake again.

In the weeks leading up to my first market, I often stayed up all night. I wanted this to work and everything needed to be perfect. I planned the display, designed the signage and packaging, and tested and retested my recipes. Only one detail was missing: I hadn't found the right apron in all of my scouring around town. It had to be perfect: elegant, nostalgic, reminding you of a warm hug from your mom, but still fashionable enough not to look too matronly.

So I decided to sew my own. I found a pattern for an apron similar enough to the one I visualized. I doctored it so it would have fuller pleats and a rustic, romantic bow. I borrowed my mom's sewing machine, picked out a dusty rose-colored linen and thread to match, and with slightly rusty sewing skills, I worked on the apron each night until the sun rose the following morning. When it was finished and ironed, I finally felt ready.

The days leading up to my first market were about the same as each one following it for the next few years, except I got faster and more efficient as time went on. I would prepare doughs and caramels during the week, designing during the day and doing my prep at night. On Saturdays before the Sunday market, I would bake all day and all night, dipping, filling, and preparing everything for the next morning. In the wee hours of the night, I would carefully iron my tablecloths and my apron, print my labels, and pack up my car with tents twice my size, sandbags, signs, and a little cash box full of change.

Once I found my place in the rows of stalls, I set up my tent and the tables just so with clean white cloths. I would line the table with long baking trays, shiny with parchment paper laid on top and sweets carefully presented on them.

Some of my favorites were the spicy, chewy ginger molasses squares, a tart lemon blueberry bar, macadamia nuts coated in a thick vanilla bean caramel on a shortbread crust, oatmeal raisin cookies with salted caramel cinnamon buttercream, and of course my chocolate chip cookie dipped in dark chocolate, sandwiching a thick homemade marshmallow. If you microwaved it for a few seconds, the whole thing would melt and settle into itself and taste like a decadent s'more.

Cake stands stacked with pastries, deliberate but not delicate, framed the entire picture, and then there was me, standing behind it all, staffing the scene in my apron and a little white folding chair for when I was tired, even though I almost never was. I smiled through the bags under my eyes, stirred and fulfilled, awakened by the hard work for something I felt passionate about.

Marketgoers would walk by, salivating at the scent of butter and cinnamon wafting toward them. I would offer a taste to entice them in, and once they'd taken a bite, I'd feel a rush of happiness as their eyes rolled back, and their mouths, still full of pleasure, would utter things that were meant for their lovers.

At the end of the market day, I would trade whatever I had left over for fresh carrots, summer squash, and raspberries from other stalls. We would chat about the day, and about what was perfectly ripe. And for the first time, I recognized something familiar in the eyes of the other market sellers: it was the same excitement I felt when I stumbled on the perfect fruit, in the perfect season. Standing all around me were others who loved the same thing: living a life full of good food.

MACADAMIA NUT BARS

This is a recipe that I adapted from a Martha Stewart recipe.
I made them frequently for the farmers' markets I sold at, and they were
so popular that customers would follow me around the city for them.

FOR THE CRUST

2 sticks plus 2 tbsp (9 oz/255 g) unsalted butter, room temperature

¾ cup (6 oz/170 g) light brown sugar, firmly packed

½ tsp (2.5 ml) fine sea salt

3 cups (13.4 oz/374 g) all-purpose flour

Preheat the oven to 375°F.

In the bowl of a stand mixer with a paddle attachment or in a large bowl with a hand mixer, mix the butter, brown sugar, and salt on medium speed until light and fluffy. Scrape down the sides of bowl when necessary.

Slowly add the flour, about 1 cup at a time, mixing on medium speed until well incorporated after each addition. Mix until the dough comes together and forms large clumps.

Prepare a 9 × 13 × 2-inch baking pan by buttering the entire surface and lining the bottom and sides with parchment paper, leaving a few inches of paper hanging over on either side. You can use the extra paper as handles to lift the bars out of the pan. Press the dough evenly into the prepared pan and prick or dock the entire surface with a fork so that it bakes evenly without air bubbles. Bake until the edges and top are light golden brown, 15–20 minutes. Leaving the crust in the pan, let it cool on a wire rack until it is warm to the touch.

FOR THE NUT TOPPING

2 sticks (8 oz/227 g) unsalted butter, room temperature

1 cup (8 oz/227 g) light brown sugar, firmly packed

¾ cup (9 oz/255 g) honey

¼ cup (1.75 oz/50 g) granulated sugar

¼ cup (2.1 oz/60 g) whipping cream

1 tsp (5 ml) fine sea salt

3 cups (12 oz/340 g) whole macadamia nuts

2 cups (8 oz/227 g) pecan halves

1 tsp (5 ml) pure vanilla extract

Reduce oven to 325°F.

Place the butter, brown sugar, honey, granulated sugar, cream, and salt in a large saucepan. Over high heat, bring the mixture to a boil, stirring constantly until the temperature reaches 243°F. Remove pan from heat and stir in the nuts and vanilla.

Pour the filling onto the crust and bake until the filling bubbles, 15–20 minutes, rotating the pan halfway through baking. You will know it is done when the nuts around the edges become mahogany-colored. Remove from the oven, and place the pan on a wire rack to cool completely.

Once the pastry is cool, lift it out of the pan using the parchment paper as handles. Use a sharp knife to cut into eighteen 3 × 2.1-inch bars. The caramel in the nuts will droop ever so slightly after the bars are cut. Store in an airtight container for up to 1 week.

A NOTE ON THE MEASUREMENTS: When I began making these bars in mass quantities, I switched to weight measurements, so I've included both in this recipe.

A NOTE ON THERMOMETERS: I've found that 243°F is the precise temperature for the bars to have the perfect consistency. Any hotter and the caramel is too hard; any cooler and the caramel doesn't hold its shape. So a thermometer is a great investment.

MAKES 18 BARS.

"GOOD" GRANOLA

{2006−2011}

GIVE ME YOUR HAND

OUT *of the* DEPTHS

SOWN *by* YOUR SORROWS.

Pablo Neruda

A GLASS OF WINE HAS 125 CALORIES, A SMALL BANANA
has 90 calories, a ½-cup serving of plain, dry oatmeal without
milk has 150 calories, and plain yogurt has about 40 calories,
which is about 100 calories less than yogurt with sweetened fruit.
I would feel a surge of pride when I bought my yogurt plain and
ate my oatmeal with water. I was in a silent war with food, and in
those moments I was gaining ground.

I exhaustively researched all the "good" and "bad" foods,
marking which were empty calories and which were worth
eating. I held a secret catalogue of nutritional information in my
mind, collected from years of obsessively reading labels and books
on nutrition and scouring the internet for strategies that would
give me the upper hand.

I allowed myself one complete meal a day, at dinnertime. To
stave off hunger, a ½ cup of homemade granola (homemade so
that I could control every ingredient), divided into two portions,
sustained me throughout the day. If I was particularly hungry—
which was almost always—I would drink matcha tea without
milk to fill the empty sensation.

I called myself a daytime vegetarian, eating small portions of meat only in the evenings, five days a week. With a ration of one dessert a week, my choices were deliberate, and I spent evenings creating desserts like chocolate peanut butter caramel tarts, which could satisfy all my intense cravings in a single bite.

To keep to a limit of 1,000 calories a day, I faithfully recorded everything I ate, from a segment of orange to a thumbnail-sized piece of chocolate, in food diaries, frantically trying to balance calories eaten with daily 10-kilometer runs.

The prize? My goal weight, my goal pants, my goal self, because whatever I was now was obviously not it. I was desperate to win, and even more terrified by what it would mean if I did.

I was in my late twenties and thin by most Western standards, but in my mind, I was never thin enough. I knew I was pretty in an unassuming fashion, but I was completely overwhelmed by all the beauty around me and in the media, a beauty I believed I should but didn't have. Every time I caught a glimpse of my body, I dissected it and myself into a hundred minuscule components and scrutinized each one, comparing them to the better versions I found in magazines, on television, in health food stores, and in yoga classes. Each time I lost this contest, and I would push myself harder by punishing myself with more starvation and sometimes hitting the parts of me I detested most until they bruised and bled.

As usually happens when things are so seemingly controlled, chaos was building elsewhere. There were too many rules. One rule avalanched into twenty, and soon there were over a hundred small balls to juggle. Inevitably, feeling exhausted by the constant effort, I would drop them all at once and would gorge on a box of saltines or a tub of ice cream. Then I'd berate myself in guilt and remorse and stick a finger down my throat and throw up until my eyes watered and my nose filled with bile. I continued forcing the finger deep down my throat until I felt like I had nothing left inside me to hate.

I lived in a perpetual state of torture, hunger, punishment, and denial for many years, not knowing what to do or how to fix it. I'd observe the girth of everyone's waist or arm and compare it to my own. I constantly debated what to eat, when to eat it, how to eat it, how much to eat, and how to burn it off. I detested myself, but even more so, I hated myself for not being able to control my obsession. And if I ever felt my clothing taut against my body, I loathed myself more. So I wore droopy, oversized clothes with elastic waists and I stopped wearing anything that I felt pretty in, because I just never did.

My disgust for myself was at its height every time I was confronted with my own naked body. After a shower I would avert my eyes from the bathroom mirror, scrambling to put my clothes back on before I could focus on my flabby, repulsive stomach. And when I did see it, I would aggressively gather the fat and skin between my fingers to gauge just how hideous I actually was. I'd cry on the bathroom floor, feeling nauseated from helplessness and yearning to be different, someone else, someone better than me.

I

ONE WEEKEND I WAS SELLING HOMEMADE SEED AND nut biscotti at the market. A frail young woman with powdery skin paced back and forth dozens of times in front of my table, inspecting the cellophane-wrapped cookies and intently asking me questions about each and every ingredient. I recognized her with her fear, her torment, her sadness. I knew her, and I knew which questions she would ask next and how she was categorizing the answers into her own columns of "good" and "bad," "safe" and "unsafe." As I watched her anguish, I remember feeling a distinct mixture of emotions I have rarely felt since: deep pity, hatred, disgust, and annoyance.

But in an instant, a strange thing happened: I realized we were the same. She was me and I was her. The negative feelings I had for her were the same ones I felt for myself. I knew that we both tortured and loathed ourselves, disciplined ourselves with starvation, and punished our bodies by forcing vomit from them. In her I saw my own undistorted reflection, and I saw how sad and scared she was, how much she longed to be told, "You are beautiful as you are." I understood her sorrow, that she sometimes cried when she was alone because the burden of feeling so inadequate was overwhelming. I knew her pain, and my heart broke for us both. I felt a spark of tenderness for the pained parts that existed in us both. It didn't make the pain disappear or heal me, of course, but it did give me a glimpse of what it was to have compassion for myself, even love myself, for one small moment.

GOOD GRANOLA

*Though I've been told that this recipe for granola is quite a good one,
I have such mixed emotions when I taste it now that I can barely be an
objective judge. Before I left for Paris, I made two large bags of this and
brought them with me in my suitcase in case I couldn't find "safe" foods
to eat there. After I returned, I never made it again.*

DRY INGREDIENTS
1,150 g rolled oats

200 g raw cashews

200 g raw walnut halves

200 g raw almonds

200 g raw pecan halves

200 g raw pumpkin seeds

200 g raw sunflower seeds

100 g ground flaxseed

400 g light brown sugar

WET INGREDIENTS
500 g honey

160 g olive oil

110 g apple sauce

5 tsp salt

2 tsp cinnamon

2 tsp cardamom

2 tsp ground ginger

2 tbsp vanilla extract

TO FINISH
175 g unsweetened shredded coconut

200 g chopped figs

200 g chopped apricots

Preheat the oven to 300°F.

Stir together the dry ingredients in a large bowl. Whisk together the wet ingredients in a medium bowl. Pour the wet into the dry and mix until very well incorporated. Pour onto 4 large sheet trays lined with parchment paper and bake for 30–45 minutes or until deep golden brown, stirring every 15 minutes.

Stir in the coconut, figs, and apricots while the granola is still hot, and allow it to cool to room temperature. Placed in airtight containers, the granola will last 1–2 weeks.

NOTE ON THE QUANTITY AND MEASUREMENTS: I would make this recipe in very large quantities. I found that it froze very well, but feel free to halve the recipe as well. Because of the large quantity, it was much easier to make this using weight measurements, so I have left the recipe the same as the original.

MAKES ABOUT 30 CUPS.

FARMERS' MARKET, PARIS

{2011}

LEAN IN TO KISS ME

IN ALL THE PLACES

WHERE THE *ache*

is

THE MOST SPECIAL.

Sanober Khan

WHEN I IMAGINE A FOREIGN PLACE THAT I'VE NEVER
been to, I tend to string together the small beads of facts I've collected over my life, and then I fill the spaces between with my
imaginations, fantasies, or fears. After a time, it becomes hard to
tell which are real and which are just my flourishes.

Before I visited, the only things I remember hearing about
France was that it had the most beautiful and sophisticated food
on every street corner (even the fast food was supposed to be
better) and that the people were unfriendly. Both of these things,
when I finally visited, turned out to be mostly untrue.

One of our first meals in Paris was at a neighborhood restaurant near our flat in the 11th *arrondissement*. It was Valentine's
Day, and G and I celebrated by eating out, but couldn't go far as
we were both only just recovering from horrible flus and were still
feeling weak. I scanned the menu and decided on the dish that
felt the most "French"—the duck confit. I'd had it a few times in

Vancouver and liked it, so I fully anticipated having my definition of the dish changed forever with this meal, leaving all other versions inedible in comparison. Instead, I got a pallid, flabbyskinned leg with a scant handful of frisée drizzled in oil that was haphazardly dribbled all over the plate, making the entire presentation seem anemic and blubbery.

And all over the city, concentrated in the tourist-dense areas, were sorry excuses for dry and wrinkly *croque-monsieur*, salads burdened with pasty white dressings lugging slices of smoked salmon and sprinkled with bits of dried chives, as if they had put rose petals on a rhinoceros and expected an elegant dance from it. I was embarrassed at the fantasies I'd so earnestly relayed to G before we left about all the beauties of French cuisine. So in complete denial, I stubbornly refused to show how disappointed I was, and I continued to eat it, giving hearty reassuring nods to G throughout each meal.

I

OVER THE COMING WEEKS AND MONTHS, I EVENTUALLY found where beautiful French food existed in Paris. I explored the nuances of the city with my mouth, forming new words with my tongue, learning the subtle language of a smile and new flavors passing my lips.

I shopped at the farmers' markets in my neighborhood like most Parisians did, Marché d'Aligre during the week and Marché Bastille on Sundays. It was here that Paris revealed herself to me first, teaching me the questions to ask to draw her story out, and allowing me to taste her character in what I thought were insignificant moments. She'd drop a word, a sigh when she thought no one was looking, and she fed me sensuously, one bite at a time.

"Un-uh-roh," said the husky man behind the vegetable stall, wearing a dirty apron over a winter coat and holding his hand out toward me.

"Pardon?" I asked, confused as to what to do next. I think I'm supposed to pay now, I had just asked for beets, he bagged them . . . now what?

His thick black eyebrows, like slugs on his forehead, rose and he looked me in the eyes and repeated himself. The movements in his mouth were exaggerated and he slowed the pace of the syllables so I could decipher them: one euro. "Got it," I thought to myself, noting the way the liaisons in the language made it both gentle on the ears and difficult to understand. And I put one euro into his fingers, which peeked through his fingerless gloves.

The vitality of the market; the sounds of conversations and food stalls; the smells of fish, herbs, onions, roasting meats; bright vegetal colors and deep earth still clinging to roots—all of these layered and piled on top of each other like books in an old Parisian bookstore.

I tasted *far Breton* for the first time, biting into the soft prunes and letting them meld with the faint scent of vanilla; the inspiring kouign amann in large wheels stuffed with roasted apples; the mature-tasting, wise crêpes made of buckwheat, educating me with their crisp edges caramelized in butter.

As I wove through the stalls, vendors would entice me with segments of clementine, the leaves still attached to the sunny skins; juicy dates, weeping their own syrup; candied strawberries, sweet and sticking playfully to my molars; and aromatic pistachios, making me crave knowledge of cultures that I hadn't wondered about before.

There were bottles of good, honest wines cared for by sturdy men wearing tweed caps with wine-stained hands and terroir under their nails, and just a few steps away, mushrooms of all kinds—black trumpets, chanterelles, morels. Their savory forest scent was trumped only by the smell of sizzling chickens twirling on a rotisserie, their juices and fat basting themselves and dripping onto a pan of potatoes embracing it. I ate the roasted chicken, simply and with my fingers.

Paris inhabited me. And I was so full of her that I simply forgot to feel ashamed of eating and being hungry.

TASTES OF THE PARIS FARMERS' MARKETS

Things you must taste at the Bastille farmers'
market on Sunday mornings:

When passing vendors, they will pass you bites. Try everything!

BUCKWHEAT CRÊPES with lemon and sugar. Try to find
a stall that focuses on foods from Bretagne, as they
will usually have the best crêpes.

JUICY MEDJOOL DATES, prunes, pistachios, and candied
strawberries from the dried fruit and nut stalls.

FORTY-EIGHT-MONTH cave-aged Gruyère
especially, but really, all the cheeses!

WHOLE ROASTED CHICKEN. Be sure to ask for the
potatoes roasted in the chicken fat.

FROMAGE BLANC bought by the carton at the *fromagiers*.
Eat with fresh fruit as a dessert.

ARTICHOKES. The artichokes in Europe seem so
flavorful and much meatier than the imported ones
I've tried in North America.

FRESH *FRAISES DU BOIS* or alpine strawberries
if you can find them in the summer.

RADISHES, with good butter from the *fromagier* and fleur de sel.

OYSTERS eaten right at the stall on plastic plates. At some stalls,
they will pour white wine into the empty shells for you to drink.

THE CONGO

{2012}

TRYING TO FORGET

DOESN'T REALLY WORK.

IN FACT,

IT'S PRETTY MUCH THE SAME AS

REMEMBERING.

But I tried to forget anyway,

AND TO IGNORE THE FACT THAT I WAS

REMEMBERING YOU ALL THE TIME.

Rebecca Stead, When You Reach Me

I KEPT SOME OF MY STORIES HIDDEN INSIDE ME FOR A long time. I would tell the ones about Paris and eating pastries until my soul vibrated with excitement, or the one of how I came to open Beaucoup Bakery. But for many years, I danced around certain memories that I held closer to me than those, if that was even possible, wary not to step on them. They weren't memories that I valued more; rather, there were simply shades in each story I didn't yet understand. So I guarded them, untouched, and some things that started out simply being unspoken became private things. Like gravity, there must be a law of nature that says that the longer a memory is silent, the further back it moves, without relevance or reason to tell it.

"When I was traveling through Rwanda to the DRC . . ." I mentioned matter-of-factly to a friend one day.

"Wait, you were in the Congo?" she interrupted.

After living in Paris for about four months, we left. G wanted to visit his sister in the DRC. She worked as a gorilla conservationist, and it was an opportunity for me to see a world that was so extremely foreign to me, even more so at the time, since I had traveled very little. I was enthusiastic to experience something different.

When we landed in Rwanda, I noticed that not only did the French language have a different sound from the one I had been hearing for months in Paris, but even the beauty was different. Bright neons and primary patterns wrapped around bodies and into fabric sculptures adorning the crowns of majestic women. I studied the yellow tulip-shaped skirts that hugged their plump and sturdy curves, and moved with rhythmic ease.

G's sister and her Congolese boyfriend were waiting for us in a car at the Kigali airport, ready to escort us across the border into the DRC. As we caught up during the four-hour drive, I observed the landscape. Bright metal shacks dotted lush tropical hills in multitudes of greens, a hot white light reflecting off their roofs. Women walked along the roadside with bundles balanced on their heads, and children horsed around with stained and tattered T-shirts and bare feet.

Along the way we stopped at a little general store on the side of a dirt road that sold essentials, like water, cookies, and snacks. It was dirty and dark inside, the only daylight coming through the front door. Everything was unfamiliar. The cookies were in strange and artificially bright packaging and the bottles of water looked a little dusty and dubious. After an exchange between the shopkeeper and G's sister about the actual price of the water—I was told later that there were higher "white" prices than prices for locals—we paid and turned to leave. I looked back at the shop-keeper and was startled to catch an expression on his face that was tainted with hostility.

When we arrived at the border of the DRC, it was nighttime, and I was tired from travel so I followed my sister-in-law's movements. If she went left or sat down, I mimicked her blankly. I didn't understand what was happening, so I was obedient, handing over my passport when asked, sitting there for hours while she argued with the border guards in a tiny waiting room with butter-colored walls filled with a crowd of locals. After the heated negotiation, we followed the usual process of entering the country as non-locals and slipped a few American bills into hidden hands. Then we crossed over and headed for Goma.

I

THE GROUND IN GOMA WAS LIKE A RAPID, BLACK RIVER frozen in time. A volcano had recently erupted, leaving the roads in a bad state, but no one there really cared much about things that the average North American might consider a terrifying crisis. I wondered if the locals had to prioritize their panic amid what seemed like so many other daily concerns, or if they all became numb when there was just too much to worry about.

We spent a few days watching life: eating local fruits, going to the dressmaker, socializing with UN aid workers in their "off time," drinking beer at Congolese clubs, and hopping onto the backs of "moto-taxis" to zip from one local joint to the next.

Only one person could sit on the back of each moto with the driver, and when the group of us traveled together, G's sister always kept a keen eye on where her brother and I were within the cluster of bikes, for "safety," she vaguely said. On our way home from dinner one night, we took motos as usual. I balanced on the back of one, hanging on to the driver's shirt, feeling the night air filter through the scarf wrapped around my hair and face, protecting me from the clouds of dirt. My driver fell to the back of the pack and slowed down so much that the high-pitched hum of other bikes began to soften. The driver spoke to me, asking me where I was from, turning his head back to tell me I was beautiful and that he wanted to take me elsewhere. I wasn't quite sure I understood, so I pretended not to hear and demanded he speed up. The more he persisted in talking to me and the farther back we fell, the more forceful I became, until I was nearly yelling in broken French, insisting that he speed up, *"Non! Je ne comprends pas! Allez plus vite! Maintenant!!"*

He revved the engine and the moto began to move quickly again. The others had stopped to wait by the side of the road near our home, and once the bike I was on stopped, I got off as quickly as I could, my heart pumping hard in my chest.

II

WE TRAVERSED THE COUNTRY TOWARD THE VIRUNGA mountains in search of gorillas. We sat in the back of an open NGO truck, looking out at passing parched farms and little huts, bouncing and being tossed by the wildly uneven roads. Children ran beside the truck with their hands out, asking for candy, but when they realized we didn't have any, they began shouting and spitting at us. I was startled and a little apologetic—this was a glimpse of a life so removed from my own story, but it all passed by too quickly, and I couldn't make sense of it.

On the day we planned to hike, I awoke in our small hut, zipped cozily into my sleeping bag. After a sparse breakfast of tea and dry biscuits from a package, the four of us walked into the morning light through tuber fields, headed for the base of the mountains. For eight hours, we tracked a trail of broken branches and footprints through fire ant nests, branches oozing sticky black sap, and thick, heavy brush at times coming up to my waist that we cleared just enough to pass by. After hours of wandering, we came to a small clearing. There, sitting fifteen feet away, was an animal so wild and so powerful that my frailness was immediately heightened in comparison. We didn't need to prepare for this encounter; the only rule our guides gave us just before we started our trek was to stay calm if four hundred pounds of dense muscle approached us—"If they charge, don't run, or they'll think you have a reason to."

I stood unmoving, regardless of attack or lack thereof, watching the silverback intently. All of my senses were engaged, and the adrenaline made them more acute. I took a quiet breath in and was amazed that he smelled like a human, so pungent that my nostrils tingled with the acrid scent of body odor. The sound of twigs breaking in another direction made me look away, and I saw that his band was sitting nearby. Like awkward houseguests, we observed a baby playing, the father asserting himself, mothers chewing lazily on branches.

We stood there for a long while, and finally, just before dusk, we turned to leave. We descended quickly back through the tuber fields and excited exchanges bubbled between us as we recounted the experience back to each other like children. In my broken French, a little phrase among many I fought hard to learn, *autant que* (as far as), fell fluidly from me, and I felt a shift in the way the language lived in my mind.

III

THREE YEARS LATER, AS I WAS LOOKING THROUGH THE photos of our Congo trip and was reminded of G, I remembered a funny moment we shared and then a painful one. I thought of him, something I had been afraid to do for some time. We had separated a year or two after the trip and up until that moment, it had been too painful to think of every part of our marriage and the ending of it. But for whatever reason I felt ready that day, and moments I had forgotten began to skip and dance around in my mind again. A single photo of our hut at the base of the mountains brought back memories of walking along those tall grasses at dawn, on my way to the outhouse, the sun just rising beside the mountains which were just misty silhouettes. I remembered fighting with G over some socks I had borrowed from him and unintentionally ruined on the hike. The image conjured in me the complexity of emotions the evening we slept in the little hut. The commitment I had to G, the loneliness I felt beside him, the anguish between us. These memories filled the little cracks in my past that I had refused to think about for so long to form a fuller, more honest memory. I could see that it was a beautiful one, too, because I could now remember the adventures we also shared, without the desire to forget.

TELL ME I'M BEAUTIFUL

{2012}

MUDDY WATER, *let stand,*

BECOMES CLEAR.

Lao-Tzu

. . . AND WHAT IF HE JUST TOLD ME? THREE WORDS THAT I so desperately needed to hear in the places I hide my deepest doubt. What if he did, in those moments, believe for me the thing I had no way to believe for myself . . . that I was beautiful?

These were questions that methodically cycled in my mind. I stood on both ends of the teeter-totter, getting off one end, climbing on the other, examining, covered in, focusing so intently on perspectives from all sides that my eyes felt blurry. And then, just to be sure, I would stand back, circling the entire scene to make sure there wasn't some hidden clue I had missed. Something that would give me clarity.

Maybe G was right. Maybe I shouldn't even be asking. I mean, he has a point. Maybe I shouldn't be relying on anyone for my own self-worth. Maybe it's true that by asking it is just a sign that I don't believe it for myself, and that no matter what he says, it wouldn't matter anyway. I can see that.

Does he think I am beautiful, though? Maybe it's not such a hard thing for him to say, as my husband. I hear it all the time on TV. It doesn't seem like an uncommon request.

But maybe he's right, that our society supports unhealthy behaviors like this, acting as crutches to true self-worth. And he may be right: what does beauty have to do with anything anyway? A materialistic concern that means nothing! I don't want to be materialistic. I don't want to put value on things that don't ultimately matter to being a good person. Maybe it matters too much to me, and I should stop caring about things like this.

But maybe I just need to hear it, to feel appreciated once in a while. To feel loved. At the end of the day, would it really hurt? It seems so simple; why does everything need to be so difficult?

Maybe he's tired of helping me out. I've probably exasperated him. I've probably asked him too many times. And maybe I wouldn't need these verbal affirmations if I truly loved myself. Maybe needing to feel appreciated is just a symptom of not appreciating myself. I need to appreciate myself more. I shouldn't need approval from anyone.

This cycle would continue like this with many topics. Like in the movie *Groundhog Day*, I repeated it until it felt like insanity. On and on, I tormented myself trying to gain clarity, second-guessing my second, third, fourth, fifth guesses.

"You don't know yourself as much as I know you," he would explain to me plainly. And in the end, I'd choose to trust his word over mine, not only because I simply didn't know how to trust myself, but also because I didn't even know I existed at all.

Was he right? Maybe there's something wrong with me for even wanting it. It's a serious issue I have. I need to work on this.

I

IN THE SPRING OF 2012, I WAS ATTEMPTING TO RECLAIM some form of a personal life after being so absorbed by opening the bakery. I had never been so fulfilled, and each night I slept peacefully, the way people do when they are happy. I felt empowered by this far-fetched dream that had become my reality, but I was also exhausted from devoting every single cell of my body to making it happen. Once Beaucoup was beginning to run smoothly, I decided to start focusing on my life again by taking walks, eating out, and hiring a French tutor to converse with me for two hours a week.

My tutor was a handsome bohemian from the south of France, with sharp, intricate features and a comforting, melodic accent, like a lullaby. We talked about life, the past, and painful lessons. O inspired me toward an exploration of myself in the world. Between corrections on grammar and pronunciation—*ahn-terresant, pas in-terresant*—he would ask me what my goals in life were, what I thought about love, and what little things inspired me, and I would ask him the same. We would often meet outside a covered market close to the bakery, sitting in the sun on a pier by the water. He would tell me all about the woman who broke his heart a few years before, that they were so young, and that he always regretted that it had ended. I shared with him the lessons I was turning over in my mind. I had been discovering who I was (passionate, hopeful, and flawed), the person I ached to be (still passionate and hopeful, but perhaps a little less flawed), and was struggling to get there as quickly as possible.

In the years I was depressed, I lived much like a shadow, and after that intense struggle, when I eventually shed the heaviness of it, I was determined to never go back.

But I was impatient. I worked incessantly to watch, analyze, and correct myself; I learned everything I could and worried that if I stopped for a moment I would never get there, wherever "there" was. I was running as hard as I could toward happiness and wholeness because it made me feel alive, but also to try to get to the place where depression wouldn't find me again. When I spotted slight flaws in my happiness, I would become disheartened, but I still forged ahead.

"Do you know the meaning of the word *apte*?" O asked me one afternoon in French, as we chatted at length about the act of learning in life.

"Is it the same as the English word?" I responded in my wobbly French.

"*C'est un peu différent*. One can have knowledge and one can have skill, but to be truly capable of living it, the understanding must reside in one's body. Sometimes it is not up to us when we can finally live the lessons we know in our minds; it must reach our heart."

The moment I heard this, I stopped running. I felt the small muscles that were shouldering the disappointment, guilt, expectation, and determination to be happy simply let go and rest in détente. The word *apte* seemed to give me precious permission to live, exactly as I was, in the space between *here* and *there*.

"I can only do so much," I thought, realizing that no matter how hard I tried to run from the darkness, toward the light, no matter how hard I worked to get away from my fears, to force my mind, to control my desires, to learn, to change myself, to be, life had its own timing and its own wisdom.

I let go of the breath I had been holding for so long. Apte.

Years later I reminded O about this word engraved on me like a tattoo, but he barely remembered the conversation. Amusing how a passing comment to someone can become an entire world that another inhabits, informing the way they see. We laughed at our differing memories, chalking it up to a combination of my flawed French and my lush imagination, which created the meaning behind this beautiful word that I've held on my lips for so many years. *Apte*.

II

I WAS DOING EVERYTHING IN MY POWER TO MAKE THE marriage work, including begging for counseling, reading self-help relationship books on my own, assuming the blame, changing, shifting to any position, any place . . . just to try. I remember pleading with G one night, "Please, if there is anything I can do, say, be, let me!" But there was nothing, just a sad, silent emptiness, still in that stale room.

I tried everything, and everywhere I went I hit a wall. I didn't know what else to try, and I was exhausted. So in our last year together, I took one last shot. I took a step back, switched gears, and took a logical, pragmatic approach: I suggested that we check in each week, every Monday evening, to brainstorm ideas on how to save our failing marriage. I managed this approach as if it was a project with goals, action plans, deliverables, and key indicators of measurable success. I recorded minutes for the meetings and performed follow-ups for accountability. But it didn't take long for me to sense that my ideas were dismissed, and deliverables were left incomplete, with only pages of minutes saved on my laptop as evidence of the efforts.

III

"WHAT DO YOU WANT FROM ME?"

It was the first time he had ever asked me this question. It signaled the breaking of his own pride, that even he was admitting he didn't know the answer.

"I just want you to tell me I'm beautiful."

"I can't do that," he said simply. No pause.

I know that many people have had similar experiences in

relationships. They try and try, beyond what they thought was even possible, and then one day, like the sound of a small twig breaking, a switch flips, and they know it's over, that it's out of their control.

After breaking apart the puzzle of our marriage and reassembling it in countless ways, a thought finally settled in my body, one true thing I didn't need to dissect: I had needs. I needed to feel like I was beautiful to the man I loved. I needed to be met halfway, for my needs to be acknowledged and respected. I saw that I could not force G or anyone to understand; I had no control over it, and no longer needed to. Wrong or right, I didn't have to justify my needs or fight for the right to have them.

I believe, as much as I can, that G was genuinely trying to love me in the only ways he knew how. And because nobody is ever a perfect saint or sinner (neither of us were), our good intentions, love, fears, shortcomings, and desires were just blended together like muddy water, and we could not love each other with the clarity to make it work.

A RECIPE FOR CLARITY

1 cup muddy water

Place a cup of muddy water in a quiet place. Wait for as long as necessary for the silt to settle to the bottom and for the water to become clear. Repeat when clarity is needed.

LES PARISIENS

{2011–2013}

AUCUNE CIRCONSTANCE NE RÉVEILLE
EN NOUS UN ÉTRANGER DONT NOUS
N'AURIONS RIEN SOUPÇONNÉ.
VIVRE, *c'est* NAÎTRE LENTEMENT.

Antoine de Saint-Exupéry

EARLY IN THE SPRING OF 2011, G AND I ARRIVED IN
Paris, and I began to teach myself French. I was using books and
podcasts but mostly learning from being surrounded by the language. Yet it wasn't the French that I had nearly failed in high
school, where conjugations of subjunctive verbs dominated conversations, rendering them tasteless and practical, like dry bread. No,
this French was juicy and warm, and solitary words painted sensuous stories, like the words "peach" or "woollen" do in English.

I would wake before dawn each day, shower, put my wire-framed glasses on, and pull my hair back into a tight bun, neatly
set at the nape of my neck and parted precisely to the right side.
I gave little attention to a mirror other than to check for anomalies. I put on what my hands could decipher in the dark, not
wanting to disturb G's sleep: socks, jeans, a T-shirt. Then I packed
my clean and pressed chef's uniform into my bag before walking
under purple skies to catch the metro to pastry school.

It was among my favorite times of day, sitting on a rustling
underground train early in the morning. I would use the reflections

in the inky glass to spy discreetly on Parisians, sleepy-eyed with elsewhere thoughts: of previous nights, stressful workdays ahead, or of a budding love or waning marriage. I loved to guess about these while I sat listening to French lessons on my phone and reading the daily subway papers, looking up words I thought looked important or pretty to say aloud. *Ensuite*, next. *Pousser*, to grow. *Sympa*, cool! *Interdit*, forbidden.

I always arrived early at school to avoid fighting with the boys over the only change room, hoping to bypass the awkward accidental walk-ins that happened frequently. The school always smelled of a mixture of freshly applied French cologne and pastries baking in the oven first thing in the morning. Every day there was something different to taste, left over from classes the day before, and I always hoped it would be *pain au chocolat* or *gateaux aux marrons glacés* (I am still partial to them).

Each week we welcomed new students, chefs from around the world at the top of their profession who came to our school to be taught by the teachers who had attained the sacred titles of *Champion du Monde* or *Meilleur Ouvrier de France* (or MOF's as we would call them for short), one of the highest designations for trades professionals in France. We in the *longue durée* or extended program spent three months seeing chefs come and go, clowning around, feeling a bit like an elite family with the small group of instructors, and developing a sense of pride that I imagined secret societies have.

At thirty-two, I was the oldest and the only native English speaker in our small class. Learning beside me were five other students mostly in their late teens or early twenties: two Parisians; a Spaniard; a Colombian; and, a petite Vietnamese woman, H, with such an air of adolescence that it was hard to know how her two-year-old child had exited from her tiny frame.

Every day at noon, after morning lessons of *pâtes* and *crèmes*, we would pull out a makeshift table and chairs and spend an hour and a half eating lunch together. On the first day of class, when they announced our lunch break, I thought to myself, "An hour and a half to eat? What am I supposed to do with the other hour and fifteen?!"

But I fell into the pace, and instead of just eating lunch, I enjoyed eating leisurely with my classmates. I got to practice my French, and over time it improved from broken, caveman-like sentences to ever-so-slightly more elegant lines.

I always had with me a salad of mesclun, lamb's lettuce, or frisée from the farmers' market, topped with slices of ripe, ready beets, plump carrots, new varietals of apple, and other foreign and exciting things, like black radishes or *tomate coeur de boeuf*. I took my time appreciating each bite, marveling at how my salads tasted so intriguing with all these new textures and flavors. Afterward, we would lay out an array of pastries that other teachers had made that week, bisecting each to inspect their profiles, and evaluating them, aspiring to an air of knowledge and scrutiny that we had not yet developed.

I

IT FELT LIKE A BURST OUT OF NOWHERE, BUT I KNOW IT was just another word my body had been learning. It started with a handful of letters slowly collected over time, which then formed sentences that spoke of falling in love.

We were learning the complex language of chocolate that week in class. Our instructor, J, in his mid-twenties, was particularly well known for his incredible palate, and had been awarded prestigious titles for his talent. With a decisive hand and innately delicate movements, he created the most awe-inspiring show-pieces and sumptuous bonbons, possessing the artistry of balancing beauty and flavor that few do.

As we gathered around to watch our first lesson, my throat suddenly became hot, and I felt the temperature of my fingers rise in contrast to the cool, hard marble slab they rested on. For a split second I puzzled at these unexpected symptoms, scanning my body in search for illness, but stopped when I realized that my eyes had been locked on J as he demonstrated how to temper dark chocolate. In its final stage, it needed to be precisely thirty-one to thirty-two degrees Celsius, just shy of body temperature. He slid and swept the melted chocolate over the table, then dipped a thin palette knife into the shiny pool and touched it gently to his lower lip, pausing for a moment in contemplation to feel the warm chocolate on him and then licking it off when he had successfully gotten a gauge.

I remember my lips growing slightly numb in desire before I pulled my gaze away nonchalantly for composure, with an ache in my body.

I I

I SACRIFICED A LOT TO GO TO PASTRY SCHOOL. BECAUSE this was my one opportunity, I was a voracious student, letting every question spill out of me, ignoring my insecurities, and devouring the answers. All of my senses engaged, I held snowy *tant pour tant* in the palm of my hand and rubbed sticky *pâte à choux*, raw, between my fingers. I documented everything in copious notes and drawings, creating my own shorthand language for common kitchen words like *congélateur*, *frigo*, or *douille*. The smells and sounds of the kitchen sunk into me, and I squealed,

oooo'ed, and laughed freely when pastries puffed, crisped, bubbled, or jiggled.

At the end of the week, all the components of the dishes were
assembled, and we created a display with each pastry laid out in
neat little rows to present to the school with a *dégustation* to follow.

Dégustation: nom féminin. 1. [par un convive] tasting

This new word settled in my belly. I learned that there was a
difference between the act of eating (*manger*) and this act of tasting. In French, the two are rarely used interchangeably.

Of all the pastries we had created, I couldn't have imagined
that the *baba au rhum* would be my favorite. It looked like a
bloated, bready doughnut with a curl of *crème Chantilly* placed on
top as its only attempt at beauty. We were told to keep one aside for
F, our school director, as it was his favorite. That fact was enough
for me to try the baba au rhum first amongst the dozens of more
appealing and elegant-looking choices. I forced my spoon into its
tan skin. It relented slightly, moisture releasing from the pressure,
and I dipped the morsel into the cream before placing it in my
mouth. The syrup-drenched cake flowed with juices of vanilla,
rum, and passion fruit from its tender crumb, and the creaminess
held the entire experience on my tongue for a moment longer.

III

MY CLASSMATES WOULD LAY A HAND AT THE SMALL OF
my back and lean into me, and I, completely unprepared for the
French *bisou* (or *bise*), would step away, assuming they needed
to get past me. Their faces would turn red in embarrassment
and confusion. J witnessed this and explained with an amused
chuckle that they were trying to greet me "good morning" with
a kiss on my cheeks. Sincerely flustered and not understanding

how the two connected, I replied, "But kissing is reserved for my husband."

The teachers began to tease me, pretending it was their birthday and insisting that it would have been insulting in the French culture not to have a kiss from me.

Even though I eventually understood the gesture, I secretly dreaded the day it would be genuinely asked of me again. "How do I get so close to someone's face and move to the other cheek without accidentally grazing them on the lips? And how do we know which cheek to start with first? And where do I put my hands?" I anxiously wondered. I fabricated nightmares about all the disastrous situations that could happen with my repressed awkwardness manipulating my movements like a clumsy marionette.

IV

I REMOVED MY TUBE SOCKS, BAGGY JEANS, AND T-SHIRT and replaced them with even baggier pajamas, thicker socks, Birkenstock sandals, an old fleece sweatshirt, and a hoodie stained with neglect. I settled in next to G to eat dinner on the uncomfortable European-sized couch.

"What do you want to watch tonight?" he asked, as though in a well-rehearsed skit.

"I don't know, maybe *Grey's Anatomy* . . . or a movie?"

"Which one haven't we seen?"

G and I were continuing our usual dance, only now in France, I would try to improvise the steps a little, feeling adventurous and asking him if we could go out to explore a covered market, new restaurants, or a pastry shop some nights.

He spent his time alone in Paris, often meditating the entire day and not leaving the flat until it was time to meet me at the train station each afternoon after pastry school. On weekends, he would sleep in and continue meditating, which gave me as much time as I wanted to explore the city alone on foot. I traveled to all areas of Paris, seeking to confirm rumors of the best croissant or pastry. Eventually, I found my own dances and created private rituals for myself: coffee and pastry at Carette in the Place des Vosges on Sundays and roaming around the bustling Le Marais neighborhood, exploring its quaint shops and street performers. I would wander, getting lost, and delight in the different street names, like Rue des Blancs Manteaux (Street of the White Coats) and Rue des Mauvais Garçons (Street of the Bad Boys). I would walk into the stores and run my hands along the beautiful clothes, admiring how effortlessly and seductively French women wore their fashion.

In the evenings, after long days of studying the city, G and I would find ourselves in our usual bedtime procedures. Teeth brushed, faces washed, lying in our separate beds, turning off the lights with a customary "good night." And I would lie there, playing over all the new words I had learned that day and feeling incredibly scared and guilty about all the dreams that I believed were plainly "unsafe" for a married woman to have.

V

"*LA FEMME VIENT!*" SOMEONE WOULD SHOUT—THE WOMAN
is coming.

I didn't catch the words, but then a few of my instructors
would casually stroll to the front door as I walked past, and I
would look around me, seeing nothing and wondering what the
fuss was about. So I continued walking as their eyes followed me.

Spring had arrived and, in admiration of the enigmatic
beauty of the French, I began attempting to mimic their ways. I
left my long hair tousled in curls, hanging down by my waist, left
my glasses off, and picked my dresses for their casual elegance,
ones that clung slightly more to the sloping curves of my body.
Since it was all so new, the thought never crossed my mind that
the instructors had come to admire me.

After three long months, school was coming to an end, and I
felt different. I was outgoing and friendly, chatting with new students, cracking jokes, and taking playful jabs at my teachers and
classmates. A few of the teachers, men still much younger than
me, would playfully ask about G and jokingly suggest a rendez-
vous. I laughed at the preposterousness of the idea, never once
taking them seriously and assuming they were trying to be funny.
When they told me I looked beautiful, I automatically believed
that they were joking.

A few days before school ended, J told me he had an important secret to tell me. I laughed, and when he said he would tell
me on the last day of school, I joked back, "If I have to wait, it
better be a good one because I don't like being disappointed."

On the final day, I had a sharp, bittersweet feeling in me. I
hated the thought of leaving school and my new friends, but I
wanted what came next, my *stage* (internship) and my upcoming

travels around Italy and France. I'd had so much fun, learned so much, been so immersed in my passion, and opened up as a person. I felt like I was leaving a precious period of my life behind.

J seemed to be extra gregarious that day, and as everyone gathered together after our graduation ceremony, I teasingly asked him in front of everyone what his secret was, not thinking he really had one. He went quiet and replied in French without looking at me, "Just that all the girls look beautiful today."

"*Évidemment!*" I said smiling, thinking it was another joke, stopping only to detect his crestfallen face. Although I registered that he looked embarrassed and walked away, I didn't understand and didn't think much more of it.

Just before I left, I found J in the classroom by the door. When I went up to him, he leaned in, gave me a bisou on the cheeks and quietly said goodbye to me.

"How do you feel about what happened with J?" my class-mate, H, asked me after we had found a place to stand on the busy metro home.

"What do you mean? What happened with J?" I tried to recall anything out of the ordinary.

H looked up at me through her arched eyebrows. "Don't you know that J has feelings for you?" she asked.

"What? What do you mean by that?" I thought I had mis-understood H, with her Vietnamese accent.

"J likes you. It has been a while now. It's obvious; he talks about you all the time when you are not in the room." My brow furrowed from trying to piece together the story. "Haven't you noticed?" she added in the silent space.

"It's not possible," I said quietly. But deep down I knew she was right. I took a moment to wrap my mind around how enor-mous it felt to be desired.

That night, and for a week afterward, I couldn't sleep. My heart throbbed and pumped as I continued to put the story together. The regret—how could I have not known? God! If only I knew! My blood boiled with desire to go back to that moment with J, to have said something different. I was angry at myself for not seeing it sooner. And each time I thought of it, my insides crawled with lust for him.

VI

WE RETURNED HOME FROM EUROPE, AND LIFE RESUMED as it was before, but I still felt changed. I felt surer of myself, my own beauty. My time in France was a little like cleaning a dusty mirror. Each time I indulged a passion or curiosity with all my senses engaged, when I was touched by all the beauty that I saw in the architecture, food, language, and people, and when someone said that maybe I was beautiful too, there in the mirror I could see my own clear reflection and I believed it.

When the holiday season came, I decided to test a far-fetched theory, that maybe I wasn't as thoroughly to blame for the fact that G and I rarely had sex in the past eight years of our relationship, that perhaps I wasn't as damaged as I was made out to seem . . . and in part, I didn't have much to lose anymore. So I came up with an idea. Instead of some piece of kitchen equipment and a food magazine subscription, this year I would ask G for lingerie—red, lacy, and as hot as they made them. He seemed confused by my boldness, offering me a simple "sure" and nothing else. I'm not sure what he thought of it. I didn't care.

So Christmas came. I opened my gift, and I picked an evening when he would be home. I walked around the house with nothing on but a see-through lace bra the color of holiday gifts and a matching lace thong. And then I walked past him in the hallway on his way to the kitchen. Stunned, he stared for a slight moment longer, and then proceeded to ignore me for the rest of the evening.

VII

AFTER THE BAKERY OPENED IN 2012, I WAS EXHAUSTED and, on a whim, went back to Paris. It was the only place I knew that could revive me. I decided to take a week-long course at my old pastry school, much like the professionals I had met so many years earlier. I walked through the front doors, and J was sitting at the desk. He looked up, smiling, and said, *"Ça va, Jackie?"* I don't remember what came next, but he described me with a word that I had to look up later: *Épanouir,* to bloom.

PASSION FRUIT BABA AU RHUM

*There is a very long history of savarins and baba au rhums, and the
difference between the two is still debated. Some say they should be made
with two different doughs, some say the baba is distinguished by the
inclusion of raisins, some assert that it is simply the shape that
distinguishes them—the baba traditionally having a cork shape and
the savarin a crown shape. Today in Paris, you often see this smaller
crown-shaped savarin sold as a baba au rhum in pâtisseries.*

FOR THE BABAS

83 g all-purpose flour

167 g pastry flour

10 g granulated sugar

5 g fine sea salt

15 g fresh yeast

50 g water, warm

150 g eggs, room temperature

80 g unsalted butter, melted

Place the flours, sugar, salt, and yeast into the bowl of a stand mixer fitted
with a dough hook, being sure to keep the salt and yeast separated in the
bowl. (Salt kills fresh yeast when they are in contact with each other, so it is
best to keep them separated until you are ready to mix.) Whisk the water and
eggs together in a pitcher and set aside.

Start the mixer on low speed and pour ⅓ of the egg mixture into the flour mixture. As the flour and egg begin to incorporate in the middle with a ring of flour
along the edge, add ⅓ more egg mixture and gradually increase the speed of
the mixer to medium, incorporating more of the flour into the egg. Once it
becomes incorporated again, add the remainder of the egg mixture and allow
the mixer to fully incorporate the remainder of the flour into a dough, scraping
the sides of the bowl and the hook as needed. Once the dough comes
together (it will be soft), bring the speed of the mixer back to a low speed and
begin to add the melted butter, little by little until it is fully incorporated. Knead
on medium speed for another 2 minutes to develop structure.

Place a piping tip ½ inch in diameter into a piping bag and fill it with the dough. Place a set of 12 silicone 2½-inch savarin molds on sheet trays and pipe in the dough, dividing it roughly among the molds. There should be enough dough to come just above the indentation in the savarin mold but not cover it. Cover with plastic wrap and allow to rise in a warm place (like your oven turned off with just the light on) until the dough doubles in size, about 1 hour.

If you are proofing the babas in the oven, remove them and preheat the oven to 325°F.

Place the babas in the oven and bake for 10 minutes; then rotate the pan and bake for an additional 10 minutes. They will be light golden brown on the undersides. Remove the pan from the oven and carefully remove each baba from the mold. Place them on a rack on top of a sheet tray and return to the oven for 10 more minutes to evenly brown the crust. Turn the oven off without opening it and allow the babas to dry for 1–2 hours or overnight. Cool them to room temperature and store in a dry place until you are ready to soak them.

FOR THE SOAKING SYRUP

1,000 g water

450 g granulated sugar

150 g passion fruit purée (I prefer Boiron)

150 g good quality dark rum

2 vanilla bean husks

3 strips of lemon peel

3 strips of grapefruit peel

Place all the ingredients in a large pot and bring the mixture just to a boil or until all the sugar crystals have dissolved. Pour the syrup into a large casserole dish and allow it to cool to room temperature. Once the babas are at room temperature, place them in the syrup in 1 layer. Allow them to soak on 1 side for a day, and then flip them to soak on the other side for another day. Keep refrigerated during this process.

A NOTE ON THE SYRUP: In order to fully saturate the babas, the recipe calls for a large quantity of syrup, so there will be some left over. You can strain the crumbs from the syrup afterward and use it in cocktails or drink it with sparkling water if you like. If you have leftover passion fruit purée, it can also be used in cocktails. I also like to make a curd with it: try using it to replace the lemon juice in your favorite lemon curd recipe.

FOR THE CRÈME CHANTILLY
500 g whipping cream
40 g confectioner's sugar, sifted
Seeds of 1 vanilla bean

Whisk together the cream, sugar, and vanilla bean seeds until the cream creates stiff peaks. Place in a piping bag fitted with a large star tip.

TO ASSEMBLE
A bottle of great aged rum

Place 1 heavily soaked baba in a shallow bowl with the well facing up. Drizzle with a few tablespoons of the remaining syrup. Pipe a rosette of crème Chantilly into the center of the well and serve alongside a bottle of great aged rum so that your guests can drizzle to taste.

A NOTE ON THE MEASUREMENTS: Since this recipe is a professional one adapted from my pastry school, the measurements have been indicated in weight. It is typically the way professional chefs prefer to work, especially pastry chefs, as it produces a much more accurate result.

A NOTE ON THE TECHNICALITIES OF THE RECIPE: This recipe is the same one I learned to make in pastry school except that I've adjusted the flour to compensate for North American characteristics. If you are in France, use a T55 flour. I've specified using savarin molds, which you can buy online or at E. Dehillerin in Paris, the same store where Julia Child once bought her kitchen equipment and a magical place to visit.

MAKES 12 BABAS.

THE DRESS

{2011}

BEAUTY BEGINS *the* MOMENT

YOU DECIDE *to be* YOURSELF.

Coco Chanel

WE ARRIVED IN PARIS ON A DARK NIGHT AT THE END OF winter, hungry and displaced. We climbed the sagging steps to the little apartment we had rented on the second floor in the 11th *arrondissement*. I had spent the last few weeks learning French, so I mustered the courage to go order a pizza from the Italian restaurant below. Four patrons leaned against the walls and counters, waiting for their dinner, while a portly Italian man pushed pies into a wood-burning oven and gruffly took orders through a little window.

"*Un pizza avec jambon, s'il vous plait,*" I said, slow and childlike.

"*Surplaceouàemporter?*" The reply so quick that it sounded like a single, impossibly long word.

I paused, unsure of what to say next. I hadn't learned this one. I had studied for a month, focusing on verb conjugations and words for kitchen utensils, a crash course before leaving for Paris. But nothing had prepared me for the speed and cadence of the language in its native home.

A young man, precisely dressed in a wool coat and scarf, turned to me as my panicked eyes met his and politely translated. "He's asking if you'd like it for here or to go."

As I ate the pizza in our apartment that evening, I was

overtired from my travels, but my stomach churned with worry and questions. "Will I like it in Paris? Will I be mortified every single day? Will G hate it here? Will he hate me for bringing him here? How will I order food again? What were the words for 'for here' and 'to go'?"

The following morning, my questions were pushed aside by my excitement to explore. I put on a baggy black sweater, loose yoga pants, rubber boots, and a thick parka, a comfortable winter uniform I was accustomed to wearing during Vancouver's rainy season. It was definitely not an ensemble chosen for its stylishness, or even one that I particularly liked. It was a default outfit. Living with a tightly controlled budget, I made purchases carefully and with practicality, but mostly my clothes were chosen to avoid the discomfort I felt with my own body. I had come to despise it— my arms, thighs, and stomach felt like unwanted houseguests. When a waistband pinched me or I felt the fabric of my clothes moving on my skin, they were disgusting reminders that I indeed had a body and that I wanted it to be so different: smaller, harder, more beautiful.

I emerged from my new apartment and was immediately confused by the equally confused stares directed at me. Suddenly I found myself a guest in a city, obliviously walking the streets of Paris in what the French would consider a housecoat. On the metro, I observed women of all ages thoughtfully presented, each article of clothing considered. I watched a graceful woman in her sixties stand with elegance and ease, wearing a fur coat as casually as if the fur were her own. My eyes followed seams downward toward the ground and I saw a sea of shiny leather, clean and respectable, not a sneaker or rubber boot in sight. I felt ashamed and realized that, here in Paris, there was no room for my self-loathing.

Over the course of the four months we were in Paris, I curiously watched as women strolled down cobblestone streets, walking with an entitlement to the sway of their hips. It was not only the young women, slim and tall, but women of all ages and shapes. Each seemed to strut with a rooted knowledge of her own beauty. I wondered about women who were fatter and stouter than me, envying their beauty and investigating its source. I spent many afternoons admiring the old works of art in the Louvre and adorning the Paris streets, noting how the bodies in these beautiful sculptures and paintings were not at all what I had been telling myself I should look like. They were not tiny, with flat stomachs and frail-looking limbs; they were voluptuous, sensual, and strong. Their bodies hosted elegant movements, and their stomachs, breasts, and legs looked a little like my own. My watery ideas of beauty were slowly being rendered tasteless by new, richer, and deeper ones.

So I tried it. I imitated their walking with my own unrefined movements, slowly discovering that the sway of my own hips came naturally when my shoulders were not hunched and shy. I began to inhabit my own body, claiming ownership of the space it took in the world.

With spring came my birthday, and the damp sheen of a wet Paris winter was replaced with bright blue skies. The trees began to fill in with bits of young green, making sense of their boxy shapes. As I walked through the Place des Vosges on a Sunday, as I did every week, I noticed that locals who had been hibernating indoors emerged with the verdant colors and textures. I was seeing a new side of Paris, one that was vibrant and lively.

I decided to use some of my savings to buy a new outfit for a dinner I had planned with G to celebrate my thirty-second birthday. After days of looking, I walked into a boutique and hesitantly picked out a few pieces that caught my eye. One was navy, long-sleeved, and with a boat neck and a low-cut back. I tried it on. It reminded me of something a French ballerina would wear. The other was a cream-colored dress with a scalloped detail, and with each I quietly asked the salesperson what she thought when I stepped out of the change room, trying to decide between the two. She would reply each time with one eyebrow slightly arched, "Well, which do you like?"

I became frustrated with her ambiguity and blurted out, "You're the expert; aren't you supposed to tell me if they look good?"

"It's on your body; aren't you supposed to know how you feel in them?" she retorted.

I paused as her words fell into place, and then I finally understood. I understood what made all those women I admired so beautiful: it was that they *felt* they were. It was true. It didn't matter what anyone thought; if I *believed* I was beautiful, then I simply was.

I looked at myself in the full-length mirror and saw a pretty girl, with an elegant face and slender legs peeking out from the hemline. My eyes were drawn upward to the dress hanging from my olive-skinned shoulders, smooth and broad, the fabric cinching at the narrow curve of my waist and the scalloped edges framing my breasts. What I saw was quite beautiful. And that day I began to see myself as beautiful too.

So I left the boutique with both dresses.

Questions to ask when deciding on a dress:
1. Does it make you smile?
2. Do you feel beautiful?

ITALY

{2011}

EVERYTHING YOU SEE,

I OWE TO *spaghetti.*

Sophia Loren

I ASSUME THAT WHEN YOU MOVE TO A NEW COUNTRY with a new culture and new customs, at some point you arrive at that funny place where you are no longer considered a tourist, but not yet a local. It's probably much like when the honeymoon phase with your young red-hot lover is over, but they have yet to mature and grow into a part of your real life. You see their dirty socks lying on the floor and the open bag of potato chips on the kitchen counter as you try to make a smoothie in the morning before heading out to an actual job. It's that place where you realize you're no longer getting the best of any world.

By the time pastry school ended and G and I had been in Paris for several months, that's where I was in my relationship with the city. And though I truly believe Paris and I would have worked it out eventually, I was quite relieved to get a change of scenery.

We were going to explore Italy for a month. I'd heard so much about the food: that it still had the rustic romance that was missing from Parisian cuisine, the sun-ripened, just-picked-from-grandmother's-garden, terroir-obsessed dishes that we all dream will change our lives and make us seem much more worldly.

I was drained from school, so we booked a two-week tour

that covered much of Italy, but we planned to explore the remainder of the country on our own afterward, when I had recovered. I was careful not to book a tour marketed toward college kids, which I imagined would involve drunken nights and nineteen-year-olds wanting anonymous Italian experiences. Instead, I opted for a "high-end" one, with a heavy focus on culture and churches.

Our hotel in Rome was a garish interpretation of mid-century modern design, as if the design had unbuttoned its shirt and put on some thick gold chains to nestle in its chest hair. We checked in and waited in the lobby for the rest of our new tribe to arrive. One by one, the couples and singles we would be spending our next weeks with started to populate the bright gold, orange, and green mirrored lobby. No one was a day under sixty, and some were closer to eighty. In trying to avoid a party bus, I had gone to the opposite extreme and unwittingly booked us into a tour for retirees. I noticed they were as puzzled as we were by the entire situation, but it didn't take long for me to get into the pace, although it was a touch slower and stiffer.

While there were some obvious restrictions on our travel, such as the difficulty of using canes on cobblestones and trying to get in and out of gondolas in Venice, there were many meaningful conversations about life that might not have been possible with kids on their way to being black-out drunk, and I felt helpful when answering questions about "cellular technology" and how to get our travelmates' wireless working so they could send updates to their grandchildren.

In the moments I felt particularly bored, I secretly loved to antagonize a misogynistic retired psychotherapist who attempted, on many occasions, to analyze me, but not as discreetly as he would have liked to believe. He would inevitably become frustrated when I would playfully analyze him back, and yelled through his teeth with a face that the word "huffy" was truly created for, "What!? You are trying to analyze the analyst?!" I'm not sure if it was too cruel of me, or if years from now I'll be embarrassed by the childishness of it, but it did make me laugh and satisfied my sense of rebellion and cheeky fun.

I

ITALY WAS POWERFUL AND DIRECT, AND ITS FLAVORS, tastes, and sounds struck me to my core in the same way. As G and I traveled through the country, I collected these seemingly scattered moments, and when placed side by side, they formed a rich memory.

(ROME)

I tasted a squid ink pasta, coated gracefully in a deceptively simple red pepper sauce that tasted as if it had been simmering gently on a stove for days, but also offered the verdurous taste of a ripe pepper picked that morning.

(BOLOGNA)

There was everything and then gelato. I had tasted the best of them across the country, but in this city, we found a place called Cremeria Funivia. For me, the best flavor was the "Alice," a smooth mascarpone gelato nestled in a cone with some melted chocolate that oozed out as you bit into the last of it.

(SICILY)

After seeing what felt like the hundredth church, our tour stopped in a little courtyard, and we all sat in the shade out of the hot sun to eat cannoli. The interior of the crisp shell was coated in dark chocolate, and when I bit into it, the cold, slightly sweetened ricotta filling gently yielded. It was the first and last time I have loved a cannoli.

(NAPLES)

In many life scenarios, there are no other reasons required other than pizza, and this is the best example I have. G and I took a three-hour train to Naples, had five hours in the city, and visited only three places: Pizzeria di Matteo, Il Pizzaiolo del Presidente, and Pizzeria da Michele, eating a Margherita at each. It was as you'd imagine: an airy and chewy crust with a delightful char encircling an intense tomato sauce dotted with creamy *mozzarella di bufala*. Yet it wasn't the pizza (or the sheer amount of it that we ate that day) that lingered in my mind long after we left, though I do still remember its taste. Instead, I recall it being the first time I felt threatened in a city. I'm not sure if it was the plaza filled with garbage and dirty mattresses, the hard-looking men who refused to break eye contact, even when my eyes turned downward in submission, or maybe that I had a sudden awareness of my naïveté in contrast to the aggressively searching stares around me. I just knew I wanted to eat pizza and leave.

(MODENA)

A drop of 150-year-old balsamic vinegar, pitch-black and as glossy as tar. The owner of the vineyard sensed my passion and offered me a taste that he himself rarely took. He explained to me that his great-grandfather, who picked its grapes and started aging it, also knew that he would never taste the fruits of his labor. I had never heard of such belief in and love for the process itself.

(BOLOGNA)

The Italian aunties were teaching me the importance of making a fluffy gnocchi, and this was a part of it. We roasted potatoes in a pan of salt, drawing out as much of the moisture as possible. Their hands guided me, picking up where I was slow and concealing my errors. In the end, feathery white pillows drifted onto a plate in front of me and I was told to eat. They melted like clouds on my tongue.

(SIENA)

I wanted to see it with my own eyes, sienna earth, the color that inspired so many. I saw a charming wine barrel sitting in front of a little store with charcuterie hanging from ceilings and colorful jars lining the walls, and it all invited me inside. Two of the friendliest and most fun-loving Italian men stood behind a counter, one with a large mustache and the other a little less gregarious-looking, welcoming us. I indulged in hours of passionate discussion about food, tasting everything cured and dried that made them sing, and I relished it all. In the end, they sent me away with a bottle of Chianti and I sipped from it, sitting on the ground in the hollow of the clam-shaped plaza at sunset.

(TUSCANY)

Feeling peckish, G and I bought a bunch of tomatoes and a handful of smooth apricots from a little table in front of a stone building. We walked a few steps down the road to find a place to rest and settled on a short wall overlooking rolling Tuscan hills, all lined with vineyards. I peeled apart a juicy apricot, noting how perfectly orange and blush the flesh seemed. I put half of it in my mouth and it was as though I were tasting an apricot for the first time. I plucked at the small tomatoes on their vine and they were sweet and rich and still warm from the sun. I looked out, the undulations of the landscape becoming more subdued as they fell into distance. I was moved, every part of me, and I gave thanks.

(MILAN)

Standing inside the duomo in Milan, I heard a cacophony of sounds, each resonating more deeply than the last: the low clanging of church bells, the echo of your own footsteps as you approach the sacred, reflected noises off the ornate stone ceilings, and the sound of your own whispers becoming large as if amplified for God to hear.

(MONTEPULCIANO)

The most powerful memory I have of Italy is that of a scent—so much so that it is forever fused with the country, and if I stop to imagine it, I can bring it back in its original intensity. In Montepulciano, I lay in bed reading in the late afternoon. The windows were wide open, letting the warmth of summer into my room. A breeze blew in, and carried with it the scent of chestnut blossoms. Like earthy white lilies, they had a bright, floral, grassy, creamy fragrance that filled me so that it felt like love.

RICOTTA GNOCCHI

Each time I am overwhelmed by a scent or aroma, or a faint perfume
drifting by, I think of a dear chef I've known with a curious nose. He once
told me that he couldn't taste as well as he smelled, so he put his nose in
everything. His food was more beautiful than any I have ever known.

This recipe is from my dear friend. He claims it is the best way to
make gnocchi, and I trust him. Unlike traditional potato gnocchi, these
have a fragrant cheese flavor and a little more texture from the ricotta.
Work the dough as little as possible, as the more you work it,
the denser and more rubbery the gnocchi will be.

FOR THE GARLIC CONFIT
1 head of garlic, cloves whole and peeled
125 g olive oil

Place the garlic and oil in a small saucepan over medium-low heat. Bring the oil to a low simmer, and then reduce the heat so the oil stays just under a simmer. We want to cook the garlic slowly with low heat. Cook for 45 minutes to 1 hour until the cloves are soft but still intact. Allow the mixture to cool to room temperature and then pour into a sealable container, being sure that all the cloves are submerged in the oil. Refrigerate until ready to use. Garlic confit will keep for up to 1 week.

A NOTE ON THE GARLIC CONFIT: It may be worth doubling this recipe, as the garlic is a lovely addition to many savory dishes and sauces, adding umami and depth easily once it is made.

FOR THE GNOCCHI

800 g ricotta

100 g grated Parmesan

4 large eggs

30 g (about 2 tbsp) garlic confit

200 g + more as needed all-purpose flour

½ tsp fine sea salt

The night before making the gnocchi, place the ricotta in cheesecloth and hang it over a bowl or other container to catch the excess moisture. It's crucial to remove as much moisture as possible. Keep this in the refrigerator.

When ready to make, combine the ricotta, Parmesan, eggs, and garlic confit. Work the ingredients into a smooth paste with a rubber spatula and season them with salt.

Slowly knead in the flour until the dough forms. It will be slightly tacky. Do not overwork the dough; knead it just enough for it all to come together. The dough should have an airy, not dense, texture. Cover with plastic wrap and let the dough rest for 30 minutes.

When the dough has rested, dust a work surface with flour. Take 1 small apricot-sized ball of dough at a time, keeping the rest of the dough covered, and roll into a rope about ½ inch in diameter. Cut the rope on a slight angle into 1-inch pieces with a knife or pastry scraper and repeat with the remaining dough.

If you want the little characteristic ridges, which are great for holding thick sauces and looking pretty, roll each piece of gnocchi onto the back of a fork with your thumb.

You can freeze the gnocchi to cook later or cook them immediately. To freeze, place them in a single layer on a sheet tray and put them in the freezer. Once they are frozen, place them into a freezer bag. They will keep for up to 1 month.

To cook the gnocchi, bring a large pot of water to a boil and add a good amount of salt so that the water tastes like the sea. Add the gnocchi and stir the water immediately while the water comes back to a boil. Once the gnocchi float to the surface, take them out using a strainer and serve with an Italian ragù sauce, or panfry in brown butter and herbs.

A NOTE ON THE MEASUREMENTS: I have kept this recipe in weight measurements, as that is how it came to me from my chef friend with the curious nose.

MAKES 120 GNOCCHI (6–8 SERVINGS).

A BRIDGE IN LYON

{2012}

PROBABLY ONE OF THE MOST

PRIVATE THINGS IN THE WORLD

IS AN EGG *until it is broken.*

M. F. K. Fisher, How to Cook a Wolf,
"How Not to Boil an Egg"

IN 2002, I WAS IN MY EARLY TWENTIES, A DESIGN STUDENT on a well-worn rite of passage that necessitated a slim budget and an oversized backpack with a Canadian flag sewn on it, an amulet to ward off suspicions of being "American."

It was my first visit to France, and in search of sun and a sandy beach, I took an overnight train from Paris to Nice. I placed my burgundy pack on a lower bunk, an old map I'd bought at a stall along the Seine dangling from the side with my grey hoodie, and I lay there, staring at the bed above me and wondering who my bunkmates were.

I woke up in the morning rested. The movements of the train had cradled and rocked me to sleep more quickly than I had expected. I looked out the window to golden hills turning to fields of sunflowers. I saw Van Gogh.

I

G AND I EXPLORED MORE OF FRANCE IN OUR LAST MONTH of being abroad. We had agreed on a financial plan for the year: we each had six months and a specific amount of money to spend on anything we wanted. But since we were to pay for the other to live, enjoy, and experience alongside us during our respective six months, I planned our travels very carefully. I wanted to make sure that during "my" six months, I had enough money for us both to see and taste all the things I had only read about in books or learned about in old episodes of Julia Child's *The French Chef.* What does a "real" boeuf Bourguignon taste like? What does standing in the lavender fields of the Luberon smell like? And does Dijon mustard taste better in Dijon? (As it turned out, France imports most of its mustard seed from Canada, and so the mustard tasted, well, exactly the same as the Dijon mustard I had eaten my entire life.)

I followed a trail of dishes pivotal to culinary history, including all the Michelin-starred restaurants I could afford. I went to Brittany in search of their buttery kouign amann, hearing that no one else's compared to the original made of grass-fed butter from this dairy-rich region. We moved on to Bordeaux in search of the perfect *canelé* and to Saint-Émilion for the original macaron made by nuns, created in a place and time when almonds were a more readily available source of protein and iron than meat was. I traveled with food as my purpose, sometimes to more remote villages, knowing that I could never recreate the dishes at their best without knowing what they tasted like in their purest forms, in their birthplaces, in their terroir.

As I continued, tasting and collecting memories with my palate, my world continued to open. I ducked into every chocolate shop, boulangerie, and pâtisserie to inspect the color of the crusts, the size of "feet" on the bonbons, or the technique of their *glaçage*, making mental notes and comparing them to the next and last.

I sought out markets in every small town we stopped in, smelling the pungent, salty cheeses that made the nostrils tingle. The French language had begun to feel natural on my tongue and I spoke with ease, expressing excitement and curiosity, and bantering playfully with the farmers until they gave me bites of mirabelle, *fraises du bois*, or local salts infused with herbs or flower petals.

Every time I discovered a new flavor or texture, I would bubble over with a joy that was at first foreign but that had now evolved into a comfortable vocabulary. I allowed myself to laugh with abandon, a deep and happy sound erupting from my gut and an uncensored crack in my usual composure. It surprised me to remember that a part of me was unafraid, social, passionate, and even charismatic—things that had been slowly forgotten during my life with G.

I I

AFTER ARRIVING IN PROVENCE, I LEARNED OF AN EXTRAVAGANT restaurant at the top of Bonnieux, and the romance surrounding the stories of it took me there. G and I drove up steep, narrow, winding roads built of dry, bleached stones until we reached a perfectly manicured clearing at the top. I felt out of place in my shapeless sundress and shoes, fatigued by months of travel, so I fixed the only thing I could—my posture—and walked into the Michelin-starred dining room.

Once the progression of amuse-bouches and a choreography of glasses and silverware started, a pretty plate was placed in front of me. In the center was a whole black truffle encased in buttery *pâte feuilletée* with leafy designs made of pastry on top. It sat in a bright corn sauce that was silky on the tongue and tasted of sweet summer corn on the cob. The pastry melted in my mouth, and the truffle sat between my lips, held there like a jewel. I let the moment linger. I sat with my eyes closed for a touch longer than I normally dared to, as G had been disparaging me lately for being unrealistic and overly dramatic. G had been observing my new extroverted behavior, and it embarrassed him. His comments often implied that my inauthenticity was transparent and uncomfortable to watch.

When I opened my eyes, I looked at my husband eagerly, anticipating an equally elated reaction, but I saw only a last mouthful remaining on his plate and a bored expression on his face. He had used his delicate silver utensils as mere tools to tear apart the precious dish into manageable sizes to chew and swallow. A rock of disappointment settled in my chest, along with feelings of resentment, disbelief, resignation, and regret for a moment wasted, a beautiful taste that should have gone to someone, *anyone*, more appreciative.

"How did you like it?" I asked him, hoping I had misunderstood.

"It was OK." His usual answer.

I tried to change the subject to neutral topics. Lately I had begun to take note of interesting articles in the *New York Times* that could serve as starting points for dinner conversation. With G's refusal to speak French, everyday experiences were becoming harder to share. We ate many meals in complete silence, which anyone who has experienced this loneliness knows is even more painful than eating alone; sitting right across from me would be a painful reminder of my longing to be connected and utter inability to do so. The topic of food had become exhausting for him. He had no interest and seemed to take little pleasure in seeing mine. When I wildly tried to guess the flavors and methods of a dish, consumed in an inspiring bite, he would plainly ask me to stop talking about food. I'd feel hurt and ashamed, and I would stop, swallowing my passion.

III

FOR THAT WHOLE TRIP, WE STAYED IN TINY BUDGET hotels with dirty floors and just-clean-enough sheets, saving on accommodations because I wanted to spend as much as I could on food. Lyon was no different. I booked a small room in a hotel by the train station with blue linoleum floors, bunk beds, and a bathroom without walls. I let G choose his bunk first.

We set off to tour silk factories and walk the streets of the town, connected by intricate bridges and steep stairs. We stopped to rest on a footbridge overlooking the waterway and chatted casually about the coming months. Our time in France was coming to an end, as was my "half" of the year.

G then asked me how I planned to pay for myself to live over the next months during his half and what I planned to do with my time while I was in Vancouver. I was confused by the question. What did he mean by "paying for myself to live"? I had paid for *all* his living expenses during my portion of the year, and according to the arrangement we made a year earlier, my understanding was that he was going to do the same for me.

He explained that my situation was unique as we were abroad and so all of our living and daily expenses were considered "travel expenses" instead. Since he had decided not to travel and stay in Vancouver for most of his time, the same rules didn't apply. In short, he was very sorry I hadn't saved enough for additional expenses to live off of during "his" six months. I was speechless. I tried to understand how I had so awfully misunderstood the rules. Had they changed? Did he remember them wrong?

But what could I do? I had spent my entire budget, thinking it only needed to last the six months I was planning for G and me. I spent it, including him in everything, paying for meals he didn't enjoy, buying our toothpaste, our toilet paper. I even paid for activities like martial arts exhibitions, things I hated but knew he would like, to make his time in France more enjoyable, only to have him trail behind me like a heavy coat while I tried to explore. Now, I was left without anything to do and not a penny to spend during his half of the year.

"But I don't even have enough for a coffee with friends," I said.

"There are a lot of free things to do in the city. Maybe go for a walk instead?" he replied.

My heart sunk, knowing how hard it had been with the tight budget I was on before, before we moved, and with nothing at all, I knew it would be near impossible.

Leaning over the side of the bridge, I was angry, but I said nothing. I thought of all the moments I had wished painfully that he wasn't there with me, wasn't looking at me disdainfully, wasn't judging the integrity of my laugh, my curiosity, my new flirtatiousness with life. I ran through everything that could have been without him. I could have lived for a year in France without him, without him hating it, without him pinching off every budding dream I had to move there and live there. I longed to build a life that gave me joy, and I would have done anything to stay. But he seemed to hate France.

Then I began silently crying, knowing there was nothing else to say, no argument to make. I had simply misunderstood the rules, or they had changed—regardless, it didn't matter. There was nothing I could do, no amount of arguing or pleading would have made a difference. So I wiped my eyes, forced a big smile, and suggested we keep walking, refusing to ruin the rest of my precious time in France.

After a late dinner of meaty steaks grilled on a wood-burning fire, we headed back to our meager bunk beds, and I waited breathlessly until I felt sure G was deeply asleep. I slipped my fingers through the side of my underwear and masturbated as quietly and quickly as I could. It was seldom that I either mustered the courage to do so or that I was overwhelmed by the need, but I ended that night with a silent orgasm stained with feelings of guilt, sadness, and spite.

SUMMER TRUFFLE IN PUFF PASTRY
WITH CORN COULIS AND POPCORN

This recipe, originally named "Truffe d'Été Tuber aestivum *en Croûte Relevée d'un Coulis de Maïs et Pop-Corn," was given to me by Chef Edouard Loubet from the two-Michelin-starred restaurant at Domaine de Capelongue in Bonnieux, Provence, where it is only served in the summer months when corn is at its peak and summer truffles are in season.*

Summer truffles are usually harvested from May to August. They are not as fragrant as their winter varieties and so are more inexpensive and have a milder flavor.

Though I think Chef Loubet's version is delicious, the ingredients available in North America are often less flavorful than their French counterparts; ingredients like the truffles are much better straight out of the ground. Taking this into consideration, I've altered the recipe with the advice of a chef friend who always seems to help me with recipes concerning foie gras and truffles.

FOR THE TRUFFLES

1.5 lb unsalted butter

4 summer truffles, 30 g each

In a small pot, melt the butter on low heat and bring to a very low simmer. Brush any dirt off the truffles and place them in the hot butter to gently poach for 45 minutes to 1 hour. Remove the pot from the heat and allow to cool to room temperature.

FOR THE FOIE GRAS MOUSSE

30 g roughly chopped shallots

30 g butter from poaching truffles

3 large sprigs of thyme

1 fresh bay leaf

¾ tsp fine sea salt

¼ tsp freshly cracked black pepper

1½ tsp granulated sugar

45 g good-quality port, divided

45 g good-quality cognac, divided

100 g raw foie gras, veins removed, room temperature

1 egg yolk, room temperature

60 g whipping cream, room temperature

Caramelize the shallots with the butter, thyme, bay leaf, salt, and pepper over medium heat. After about 5 minutes, when the edges of the shallots are becoming golden brown, add the sugar and cook until the sugar melts and the onions caramelize to a dark golden brown. Deglaze the pan with 30 g port and 30 g cognac and reduce to about half. Remove from the heat and allow to cool to room temperature.

Remove the thyme and bay leaf. Pour the shallot mixture into a good blender and add the foie gras and remaining 15 g port and 15 g cognac. Blend on low speed to begin breaking down the ingredients. Add the egg yolk and cream and blend on high until the mixture is very smooth and homogeneous. Pass the mixture through a fine strainer into a resealable container and reserve in the refrigerator until ready to use.

FOR THE SWEET CORN COULIS

80 g butter from poaching truffles, divided

170 g yellow onion, roughly chopped (about ½ an onion)

75 g celery, roughly chopped (about 2 stalks)

3 generous sprigs of thyme

1 bay leaf

½ tsp fine sea salt

¼ tsp freshly cracked black pepper

60 g dry white wine

80 g truffle juice (can be purchased at specialty fine foods stores)

675 g fresh sweet summer corn kernels (about 4 ears)

2 tsp apple cider vinegar

Place 50 g of the butter, onion, celery, thyme, bay leaf, salt, and pepper into a medium pot and sweat the vegetables on medium heat. Once the onions are translucent and cooked through, add the wine, then bring it to a boil and reduce it by half. Add the truffle juice and corn, bring back to a boil, and then immediately remove from the heat to stop the cooking. We want to preserve the fresh corn flavor as much as possible. Pour the entire mixture into a good blender with the vinegar and the remaining 30 g of butter and blend until very smooth. Strain the corn purée through a fine mesh strainer, pressing well to extract all the juice. Thin out with water if necessary to create the consistency of whipping cream. Set aside until ready to plate. Can be made 1 day in advance, kept in the refrigerator, and reheated just before serving.

FOR THE POPCORN

20 g olive oil

40 g popping corn

30 g truffle oil

¼ tsp fine sea salt

¼ tsp freshly cracked black pepper

Place the olive oil and popping corn in a medium pot covered with a lid over high heat. When the kernels begin to pop, shake the pan over the heat until the popping stops for 10 seconds. Remove the pan from the heat and transfer the popped corn to a bowl. Season with truffle oil, salt, and pepper. Reserve for garnishing the dish. Can be made up to 1 day before and stored in an airtight container at room temperature.

FOR THE SALAD GARNISH

75 g rocket, oak, and/or shiso leaves

20 g vinegar

20 g olive oil

½ tsp fine sea salt

10 g truffle juice

Submerge the rocket, oak, and/or shiso leaves in an ice bath to refresh. Whisk the rest of the ingredients together in a small bowl to make a vinaigrette. Drain the salad leaves from the ice bath and dress with the vinaigrette. Set aside for up to 5 minutes until ready to use.

TO ASSEMBLE THE DISH

200 g puff pastry

1 egg

20 g whipping cream

½ tsp fine sea salt

Freshly cracked black pepper

Maldon salt

Preheat the oven to 375°F.

Roll out the cold puff pastry to a thickness of 1/16 inch and cut 4 squares, 4 inches on a side. Put a 1½–2 tablespoon dollop of foie gras mousse on each pastry square and place a butter-poached truffle in the center. Top with a sprinkling of cracked black pepper, and fold in the corners and edges of the pastry very well to seal like a little packet. Place seam side down on a sheet tray lined with parchment paper and cut a small slit in the top of the pastry for ventilation. Cut 1/16-inch strips from the remaining pastry and lay them in an X pattern on top of the pastry for decoration.

Mix the egg yolk, water, and sea salt in a small bowl, and brush the egg wash over each truffle parcel. Bake in the oven for 20 minutes until nicely golden. Let cool for 5 minutes.

Pour ⅓ cup of corn coulis on each plate, make a little pile of seasoned salad, and place a truffle parcel on top. Scatter with truffled popcorn and finish with freshly cracked black pepper and Maldon salt to taste. Serve warm.

A NOTE ON THE PUFF PASTRY: This recipe calls for puff pastry, and I think it is always better to make your own. Rose Levy Beranbaum has a wonderful recipe that has been adapted for the home kitchen in her book *The Pie and Pastry Bible*. However, making your own can be time consuming, and since this recipe uses only a very small amount, consider a good-quality frozen puff pastry, or ask to buy some raw from your local bakery.

A NOTE ON THE MEASUREMENTS: As this is a professional recipe, the measurements have been kept in weight.

SERVES 4.

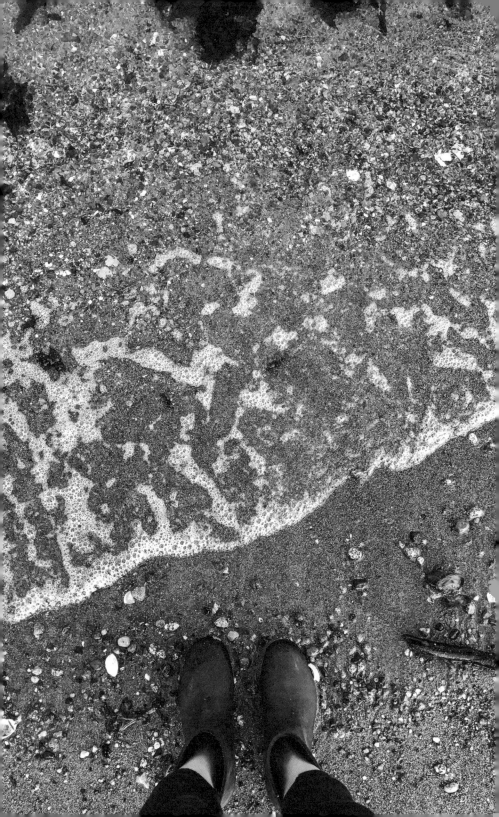

EVERY SATURDAY MORNING

{2007—2011}

I CROSSED THE *ocean*

FOR A HEART OF GOLD.

Neil Young

THE RITUALS I CREATED AT HOME BEFORE I WENT TO
France were like bolts on a rock face, anchors to secure myself as
I climbed out of depression. Visiting farmers' markets, spending
time cooking, baking, and eating; I held on to these moments as
I ascended out of darkness, and when I felt comforted or encour-
aged by them, I made a note to do them again.

On occasion, a spark would pierce through me, and the
heaviness was suspended just long enough for me to recall the
feeling of delight. And among the most meaningful rituals was
Saturday morning. I waited for it all week long. At 8 a.m., I would
arrive at a local pâtisserie on the west side of Vancouver just as
the doors opened, with a book to read, my journal, and a pen.

Each time, as though I were pausing at the summit of a long
mountain climb, I would take in the beautiful scene—rows of
croissants, sour cherry strudels, delicately adorned chocolates,
and elaborate tarts—and then I'd breathe the beautiful smells of
butter, yeast, sugar, chocolate, and coffee deep into my lungs.

I ordered the same thing every time: a double-baked almond
croissant and a latte, to stay. And since there were rarely more than
one or two people in the café at that hour, I always found a seat in
a quiet corner by the window. I had never been much of a reader
during my childhood, so as an adult, there were worlds and worlds

of books left undiscovered. There, where I could sit unhurried, luxuriously for hours, I lost myself in books, looking into other lives, hoping for answers, or to see bits of myself in a hopeful story. In some, I sought inspiration; others simply led me far away for enough time to regain the strength to tackle the next day. And between words, I took slow sips of coffee and loitering bites of croissant until I felt saturated with all of it and grateful for the reprieve it gave me.

I

AS I SAT IN THAT PÂTISSERIE, I WROTE IN MY JOURNAL, sometimes for many hours, entries upon entries, desperate to find ways to not be in so much pain; confused, asking why, asking for help, and asking myself if the pain would ever stop.

SEPTEMBER 9, 2007

We fought, I screamed. Sometimes when things get bad, I feel as if I cannot breathe, like there is no way out and it all turns within. Sometimes when he speaks, I can't even listen, I need to shut off and keep it all out. I can't handle it any more . . .

Last night I asked God for help. I said that I know he is there but I don't know what form he takes or who he is. All I knew was that he had the power to help me and that I needed it. I think (this may have only been me) I heard back, to help myself. I'm not sure why. However, I think to myself that it really does feel like I can't. I feel too far gone, too tired, too damaged. It feels too big and too much to tackle. I am burned out, tired, and on the verge of giving up. Is it realistic to say that I can do this?

I remember at a certain point in life when I attended church, random people praying for me kept telling me I was like a flower about to bloom. I'm not sure if I ever did. They would say that God would never put you through something you can't handle. But people kill themselves all the time.

I'm confused. More than confused, I'm upset and full. I'm up to my neck in negative feelings again. Everything is a fight. I need clarity in my life, decisions to be made. I feel sick to my stomach. I feel sick. I can't be this anymore. I'm not happy; miserable. No one can tell me I should be happy, or that things will get better. They won't. Hopeless. What am I supposed to do in the meantime? Until it's all over, just a waiting game until I die. Why is this worth it again? I keep trying to find some way out of this, but it's like I'm in a well. High enough to see that there could be something else but deep enough to know I can't get out. What is the point?? Why the hell am I here? If God is supposed to be here in the middle of it all then where is he? Do I have to live the rest of my pointless existence like this? I'm miserable and making everyone around me miserable too while I'm at it.

There were all sorts of lists. I wrote lists for everything, categorizing and making sense of what I felt, and the confusion within it. Lists were a way to put down on paper the things I hoped for. I wrote a list explaining what kind of mother I would want to be one day. There were sixteen points.

MARCH 31, 2010

NO. 1.   *Always hugging and kissing my kids. Even when they are teenagers and want me to go away.*

NO. 7.   *Being quiet when I need to be.*

NO. 10. *Empowering them in achieving their goals and desires.*

NO. 11. *Being an example first.*

NO. 16. *Going to their games, recitals, plays, and practices.*

I listed what I believed all my negative and positive traits were. There were thirty-seven negative and seven positive.

MAY 5, 2010

NEGATIVES:

NO. 3. *I talk too much.*

NO. 5. *I eat too much.*

NO. 11. *I am not rational.*

NO. 17. *I am too dependent on others.*

NO. 20. *I am fat.*

NO. 21. *I am ugly.*

NO. 23. *I cannot communicate.*

NO. 24. *I am not strong.*

POSITIVES:

NO. 1. *I am kind.*

NO. 2. *I like to help others.*

NO. 3. *I am honest.*

NO. 6. *I am compassionate.*

As the rest of the world woke up, I would slowly find myself surrounded in the pâtisserie, everyone needing buttery comfort and a sharp jolt of coffee. And when the café became too crowded, I would seek out the stillness again, driving to the beach and walking along the shore in my gumboots, water meeting sand. I worked hard to "get better" but was unknowingly restored by the simplest, most passive moments, like appreciating the water's blues lapping onto my feet, the mountains in springtime with snow lagging on their caps, or finding stones in pretty colors and holding them in my pocket, feeling their texture in my palm as I walked. Nature was healing me.

II

WITH EACH PASSING YEAR AS I BEGAN TO HEAL, I WENT faithfully to the very same pâtisserie, sitting in the corner and taking in all the familiar noises and scents of my sanctuary. I observed the bustle of others coming in and out, satisfaction spreading across their faces as they sipped and tasted. I noticed other solitary people looking longingly out the windows, and saw that I wasn't alone. There they were: others trying to nourish themselves in this place, in this same way.

As my obsession with baking set in, my journal entries moved away from lists of sadness to lists of fantasies, far-fetched musings about what it might be like to have my own bakery one day and what it would look like, smell like, and feel like.

III

THREE MONTHS AFTER I OPENED BEAUCOUP, DURING A trip to France, I strolled through boutiques in the Amsterdam airport to pass the time on my layover. I spotted something that I recognized immediately: a bright red journal, the same as the ones I had filled years before, before I had been consumed with all the demands of starting a new business and stopped journaling. I bought a lined journal and a pen, and on the flight to Paris, I wrote.

My desires in life: to enjoy, immerse myself with abandon, to understand the importance of my own opinion, because after all, I am the one that must live with it. Though the hardest part is to decide who I am and what I want to be. Perhaps I'll start with what I know I am now:

NO. 1.   *Smart.*

NO. 4.   *Friendly.*

NO. 5.   *Confident.*

NO. 6.   *Silly.*

NO. 11.   *Happy.*

DOUBLE-BAKED ALMOND CROISSANTS

Double-baked almond croissants were originally created to use up unsold croissants left over from the day before. They were soaked in syrup because they were stale. For this recipe, the croissants must be day-old and stale when soaked in syrup or the texture will be mushy.

FOR THE SUGAR SYRUP
250 g water
340 g granulated sugar

Bring the water and granulated sugar to a boil in a medium pot, and continue cooking until all the sugar crystals have dissolved. Transfer to a bowl or resealable container and cool in the refrigerator until cold. Can be made up to 2 weeks in advance.

FOR THE ALMOND CREAM
200 g unsalted butter, room temperature
200 g confectioner's sugar
200 g almond meal
120 g eggs
20 g cornstarch
Seeds of 1 vanilla bean
½ tsp fine sea salt

Mix together butter, confectioner's sugar, almond meal, eggs, cornstarch, vanilla bean seeds, and salt in the bowl of a stand mixer until light and fluffy. Place it in a piping bag and reserve in the refrigerator until you are ready to fill the croissants. Can be made up to 3 days in advance.

6 croissants, 1 or 2 days old

90 g sliced almonds

55 g confectioner's sugar for dusting

Preheat the oven to 350°F.

Slice each croissant horizontally. Dip each croissant half into the sugar syrup until well soaked, and place them, evenly spaced, on a rack over a sheet pan. This will help the pastries drain the excess syrup so they are not mushy inside.

Once they are drained (which should take about 10 seconds), place them on a large sheet pan lined with a Silpat mat or another nonstick surface.

Cut off the tip of the piping bag to expose a hole about 1 inch in diameter. Fill the bottom of each croissant with about 80–100 g of almond cream. Replace the top of the croissant and pipe 30–40 g of almond cream over the top and press about 15 g of sliced almonds on top.

Bake until the tops are deep golden brown and the edges look caramelized and crispy, approximately 30–35 minutes. If you notice the tops sliding off during baking, you can use a fork to slide them back on.

Remove from the oven and allow them to cool on a rack until they are warm. Sprinkle the tops with confectioner's sugar. Lift them from the pan using a spatula and serve warm or at room temperature.

A NOTE ON THE MEASUREMENTS: As this is a professional recipe, the measurements have been kept in weight.

MAKES 6 CROISSANTS.

A LITTLE KEY

{2011}

IN THE MIDST OF WINTER,

I FOUND THERE WAS, *within me,*

AN INVINCIBLE SUMMER.

Albert Camus

THE WAY THE SUN SHINES STRONG IN THE MORNINGS
during summertime in Provence would make my heart flutter,
warm with contentment. I'd go out into the light in search of
breakfast while G would sleep until the early afternoon, and I
relished the moments of solitary exploration. I liked having my
curiosity lead me, with no agenda, turning down charming cobblestone alleys if my stomach jolted with delight at the idea of it.
I liked to observe the locals on their bikes, the clothes hung out
to dry by windows, and funny bits of graffiti in French that made
me giggle to myself. I felt at peace, at home, as though I'd taken
my place in the world.

At each boulangerie or pâtisserie, I stopped to look in, doing
my usual scan for signs and signals of quality or mediocrity. Does
the crust look crisp? The crumb chewy? Are the *viennoiseries* high?
Do they use good chocolate? Is the glaze on the éclairs cracking? One morning I eventually settled on one place that had good-
looking bread. I craved a *pain au chocolat,* and although theirs
were flat and looked ill-treated, stacked one on top of another
with no reverence for its art, they had a lovely lacquered cinnamon
color, and the chocolate was still warm, oozing out of its sides. I

bought two, one for me and one for G, knowing that everything tastes relatively decent when warm.

They unceremoniously placed two pains au chocolat in a large white bag, and I walked back to the hotel to eat mine by an open window.

The sun warmed my face as I bit into the pastry. It melted in my mouth with a beautiful chew on the crumb and a pleasantly yeasty flavor from properly fermented dough. The melted chocolate coated my palate with sweet complexity and the butter infused me with its aromas, flowing into my nostrils and satisfying every one of my body's cravings.

I ate and smiled and ate and smiled until the bag was empty.

I

IN THE DAYS FOLLOWING, WE EXPLORED PROVENCE BY car, driving down winding roads with the windows down, and along landscapes dotted with wild red poppies, their fragile petals and furry stems swaying in the breeze. The warm air scented with lavender intermingled with bleached stone rose up to me like fragrant earth, and the little ancient hilltop towns with their crooked doors and streets all swirled upward to a grand church or castle.

I loved collecting my favorite cheeses, fruits, and breads from the farmers' markets that sprung from the centers of the little towns. I'd find a sunny stone step, lay out a linen napkin, and carefully arrange on it meaty olives, sweet tomatoes, and herb-covered cheese made just that morning. On the best days, I also had rosé with ice cubes floating in the glass.

It was as though I had come back to life. Each precious experience like this one was like the sounding of a deep bell, reminding me, calling me back to myself. Curiosity replaced the fear inside me, and excitement overcame self-consciousness. I was present, engaged, living, and playing in each moment instead of being perpetually lost in my mind, tangled between the regrets of my past and the anxieties of my future. I was learning to live for the things that made me happy, not for my marriage or what made G happy. I was learning to live for me.

I I

ON A SUNDAY IN L'ISLE-SUR-LA-SORGUE, I SPENT THE entire day at a flea market, picking through piles of artifacts with G trailing behind me. It was like a treasure hunt, an art museum, and an archaeological dig all rolled into one, and I refused to pass up the opportunity to explore it all. As far as I could see were row of stalls, all lining the river. Tables were filled with old linens expertly embroidered with decorative initials, a mystery I wondered about to myself. Who was E. V. or H. M.? Old post-cards sending messages of love or regards piqued my curiosity intensely, as did letters in flourished script detailing instructions on how to build a proper wall in an ancient town, an ancient house, or perhaps a church. I discovered antique surgical tools and imagined doctors muddling their way through uncharted intestines and "taking a stab at it." I flipped through old paint-ings recording family members and tried to detect in their eyes if they enjoyed sitting for the artist or thought it tedious and uncomfortable. Time-stained books, rows of silverware, serving utensils in elaborate shapes. Inquisitive about it all, I asked the vendors why there were never matching knives with the silver-ware, and they answered, "Never! People preferred to keep their own knives in those days."

I fantasized about the beautiful plates, bowls, and pitchers and about restoring and saving green copper pots and pans or refurbishing old furniture for my future home, when one day I would live there in Provence.

Among it all, I looked for something I could bring home with me, a souvenir. It had to be small enough to carry but not a worthless trinket that would be lost in a drawer one day when other memories filled its place in my mind. It needed to be important, a symbol to hold the weight of my time in France, of this moment, this feeling of happiness I'd finally found, a determined reminder to myself of the past and of my determination never to return to it.

Then I walked past an old man sitting on a lawn chair, surrounded by boxes of rusty keys in ornate shapes. There were keys the size of my forearm (they must have been for drawbridges) and ones so tiny they could unlock only secrets. I looked among them and carefully chose one that was delicate, simple but elegant with a thin oval shape.

III

BACK IN VANCOUVER, I HAD THE KEY CLEANED AND plated with gold. I strung it on a subtle gold chain to match, and immediately hung it around my neck. I held it between my fingers and felt its delicate grooves and ridges. In case I ever forgot, this necklace would remind me what it felt like to be free, to be myself.

I slowly walked home along a quiet street. It was an ordinary moment, there was nothing particularly spectacular about it, but I enjoyed it nonetheless—the warm breeze, the sun warming my skin, the cool tingling when I strolled into the shade. As I walked,

I felt my blue silk blouse graze my arms and chest as they moved with my gait. My plump and curvaceous hips pressed snug against my jeans from months of extravagant eating and in that moment, I thought to myself, "I feel beautiful." And I smiled because I knew that the thought itself was just as beautiful.

INGREDIENTS FOR A PERFECT
PROVENÇAL PICNIC IN SUMMER:

A BOTTLE OF ROSÉ WINE, chilled with ice cubes in your glass.

SALTY, MEATY OLIVES. The ones with lemon confit are very nice.

FROMAGE DE CHÈVRE FRAIS, a mild,
creamy goat cheese usually made that morning.

A PAPER BAG OF FRESH PETITS POIS. You shuck them
as you eat them, picking the little green pearls
out of their pods and popping them in your mouth.

A HANDFUL OF CHERRIES. The stems aren't necessary
but make them so much more fun to eat.

FOUR APRICOTS, ripe, tender, and blushing slightly.

A BIG RIPE RED TOMATO that looks very juicy.
(Bring a knife to cut this.)

A BAGUETTE, *bien foncée*, or well browned. There is no joy in eating
bread that is whiter than an inner thigh in the dead of winter.

LINEN NAPKINS, which you lay on your lap.
It keeps you tidy and doubles as a plate too.

A LETTER

{2016}

THERE IS NO GREATER AGONY *than*

BEARING AN UNTOLD STORY

INSIDE YOU.

Maya Angelou, I Know Why the Caged Bird Sings

Dearest,

I know you've been asking a lot of questions lately, poring over a lot of really important decisions about important topics like finding your passions, where to go, whether you should go at all, what to do when you're there, what is wrong, and what is right.

And it might even seem to you that I've got things figured out, having found passions, having gone somewhere or done something that you might consider right. The truth of the matter is that I don't have the answers either. We are in the same boat. I wonder the same things all the time; I can't see into the unknown or feel unafraid either.

If there was any difference between you and me, it might be that I have the benefit of the past: evidence. Sounds like a funny word to use, but let me explain. There was a time when I was really afraid. I thought dying would be a safer option than living, but for some reason I chose to live. And it turned out I was not devastated as I thought I'd be. All those horrible things I

expected weren't so bad after all. So, I did it again, tried
to be brave the next time I felt afraid, this time not of
living, but of failing. And it turned out so beautifully that
I laughed and jumped and danced, feeling invincible! So I
ran fast and tried it again, and that time I did fail, and it
hurt. But after, I was just fine, and it turned out I was
wiser the next time I chose to do it again.

And so you see, even though it might seem like I am not
afraid, I am, just like you. Only I have collected more evi-
dence along the way that life is good, it is safe to trust, that I
will be OK, and I am safe to trust too.

I know, because I've asked these same questions, and
know that they are all the deepest yearnings for joy in life. It
is like a song inside you that doesn't yet have notes or a
melody, and it feels painful and mournful not to have the
words to sing it. It is an honest calling to not only be happy,
or rich, or famous, or to even feel loved, but a calling to
learn what it means to love with your whole heart, without
conditions, not holding back for fear of loss, and choosing to
give yourself the experience of the fullness of life in return.
It is a yearning to inhabit the true meaning of courage.

And because you read this and know it by heart, you
have no choice but to learn what your own song sounds
like, and to sing it carefully at first and joyfully and play-
fully as you go on.

I'm still learning my song too, from the pieces I've
heard, a verse here or there, an interesting chord or progres-
sion. It sounds really pretty and makes me smile when I
have the courage to hum it.

I know it seems daunting; I know sometimes it even
seems impossible! But, believe me, because if it means

anything at all, I believe in you. I want to see you succeed and to celebrate with you when you do. And I know we all need all the help we can get, so I'll tell you everything I know to be true on this topic. But please have compassion for me. I too am learning, and my perspective often changes as I see more of the picture.

I once read that there were two ways to answer a lingering question: one, with patience, and the other, with action. I try to remember that when I feel stuck.

Joy often comes from choosing the things that bring you joy. Choosing is sometimes difficult and painful because it often means you have to let go of something old to make room for new things. Letting go can be very sad and is often difficult. Be patient with yourself, and do it when you feel ready and not a moment sooner or later. You'll know it's time when you want to more than you don't, and it comes more naturally than you'd expect.

Choosing the things that bring you joy can sometimes be tricky, and what brings you joy can sometimes change as well, making it doubly tricky. But I've found that it's crucial to have a good idea of what it looks like because it makes it easier to spot when you're making those choices.

There were times in my life that not making any choices at all was helpful too, especially when I wasn't even sure what joy looked like to me, or when I was extremely tired. Sometimes my best friend D takes me on a drive. He asks if I am in the mood, and if I agree, he drives to the prettiest places and I relish being passive, watching the beauty outside of my window change from scene to scene, being shown things I would not have otherwise known about: a quiet Japanese garden on the outskirts of the city, a

charming garden shop, a patch of autumn leaves like con-
fetti. And it was this fallow space that led me to know my
joy in new ways as I took it all in.

Be courageous in allowing yourself to hope for what
you truly want. There were times I didn't allow myself to
hope for spectacular things because I was afraid of being
disappointed. But try, if you can, to suspend those fears in
the times when you are dreaming of possibilities and explor-
ing your truest desires, even if it's just for five minutes
longer than you normally would. Because you will most
likely choose not to add every single color to your painting.
But, if you give yourself the freedom to be curious, you may
uncover something true along the way.

Once, I allowed myself to do this. When I came back
from Paris and was beginning to decide what I wanted to
do next, I sat down to imagine and allowed myself to write
a list of careers that I would want, suspending realism for a
moment. I wrote on a piece of paper:

1. *Starting a company that did culinary tours in France*
2. *Starting a bakery*
3. *Being a food and travel writer*
4. *Being a cookbook author*

At the time, I chose to start the bakery because I was so
passionate about the idea, and it was the most practical and
realistic option for me at the time. (Even though it was still
quite far-fetched!) Years later, after I had started Beaucoup
and The Paris Tours, I began to write about food and travel
and remembered this list and began to laugh. As I write
this, I am smiling and grateful because I see the goodness

and a kind of quirky humor in life. Which brings me to the next thing I want to tell you . . .

Imagine, choose, aim for that direction, work hard to get there, be tenacious, but also let it go and be grateful for what you're given along the way. Because one of the most precious lessons life has given me is that it can imagine for me much greater things that I can imagine for myself. Sometimes life can be funny: it throws us curveballs or changes directions on us, and unless we are flexible enough to look up and watch for the hidden beauty, we might miss it.

And when things are not going smoothly—because there will be times like this—try your best to be kind and compassionate toward others and, above all, to yourself. I do believe there are reasons and lessons in everything, although I know some people don't see things this way. I choose to be one of the people who do, because I see lessons all around me, and I don't see a reason to stop.

And if you are still unsure, because as you know there are very few guarantees, and it is so hard to know what you want before you see it, sometimes to know that you no longer want to be standing where you are is enough to leave. You may never find what you want, standing in places you've already looked.

Lastly: love. Love with as much of your being as you can possibly stand, because it will only make you fuller, more compassionate, kinder, more loved, and more courageous. I don't mean loving just your lovers, but anyone, everyone, the world, or life itself.

"Being deeply loved by someone gives you strength, while loving someone deeply gives you courage." When I first read this quote, I only understood that I didn't understand,

and that I wanted to. It had become easy for me to love life; I had grown accustomed to loving the world. But then I began to love where it scared me deeply to love—to love a lover. I've retreated many times, and I still do when it becomes too scary, and then I watch, listen, and look for signs that it is safe to try again. And when it is, I try it again, to love as much as my soul can possibly bear. Not for my lover, but because I desperately want to hear how beautiful my voice can sound when I sing my life's song.

Love,
JKE

THE CROISSANT

{2012}

I'VE SEEN YOU,

beauty,

AND YOU BELONG TO ME NOW,

WHOEVER YOU ARE WAITING FOR AND IF

I NEVER SEE YOU AGAIN, I THOUGHT.

You belong to me

AND ALL PARIS BELONGS TO ME

AND I

BELONG TO THIS NOTEBOOK AND THIS PENCIL.

Ernest Hemingway, A Moveable Feast

THE MORNING AFTER WE RETURNED TO VANCOUVER from Paris, I took a walk in our neighborhood, a residential area with wide roads lined with old maples and low-rise condominiums built in the fifties and seventies with aspirational names like the Villa Paloma, Casablanca, and The Chateau. It was all exactly the same as we had left it months ago, as if time had stood still. I felt alone, because I hadn't stood still.

I took a few steps along my old route but stopped abruptly. It was as startling as an unexpected clang: the silence. I heard nothing. There were no sounds of markets brimming with life, high-pitched European cars honking and swiveling in dramatic roundabouts, no chattering flâneurs or clinking cafés with their chairs lined up like seats in an auditorium, the bustling street as the performance. Paris missed me, and my heart sunk deep into my chest.

I

G DECIDED HE WANTED TO SPEND HIS PORTION OF OUR sabbatical at home meditating, which left me with a few months of solitude in Vancouver. So I spent my days recreating pastries I'd learned from school and ones tasted during my travels, desperate to bring the memories closer to me.

I hid in my kitchen, making chocolate tarts, tending to my *religieuses*, and clinging to babas au rhum, unwilling and unready to move forward. When friends inquired about our trip, I knew that they expected to hear romantic stories of life abroad, but I would only answer in monosyllables and then change the subject. I was heartsick, but I didn't know how much; I just knew I had a sinking feeling in my stomach when Paris was mentioned and couldn't bring myself to talk about it to anyone.

I hadn't wanted to leave Paris. It had changed me. The longer I was in France, the more I dreamt of staying forever, and the more I dreaded leaving. I began presenting ideas to G, ones that might tempt him to agree to living in France. Each time we took a food tour, I would suggest that I could start a similar business. I tried to convince him I was capable, and I imagined how wonderful it would be to share my passion and knowledge with others. I told him I could work as a chef in Paris, that I would work hard to support us both. I suggested opening a small North American-style bakery in Paris, since the trend for American foods like burgers, cupcakes, and brownies was becoming popular. But he never did agree, and so we moved home.

So without the hope of staying in Paris, I protected the memories of her, too precious to lose. I mourned a Paris never to be known to me again, not in the same way. I imagined visiting when I was much older, but it would be different, as different as home had come to feel to me. I was once close to knowing her so intimately, yet now I would be a stranger again. So I held this grief in my body, my arms and my hands, and I used it to create flavors and smells that we had once shared. I would cook for her, both to ingrain her more deeply into me and also to release myself from her.

II

AFTER PROCRASTINATING WITH ALMOST EVERY OTHER recipe, it was finally time to tackle the one recipe that gave me shivers at the thought of inevitable failure: *pâte à croissants*.

It was said that a "true" French croissant was impossible to create outside of France. Magnified with time like a myth, this hazy mystique of butter, water, flour, air, and *je ne sais quoi* made the croissant seem elusive and unattainable. How could one make a French croissant without French ingredients? I wasn't convinced either, and certainly didn't assume I had a better chance than anyone else.

But what galvanized my resolve to try was that I had simply gone too long without the croissant of my Paris. The one that my pastry school instructors made on Friday afternoons, the ones from the *salon de thé* that I ate with a *café crème* in the mornings. Warm, intensely buttery, savory, yeasty, slightly sour as with the best breads, light, and airy with a little chew right at the end, a shattering, cinnamon-colored, all-over-your-face-and-clothes-crust, and a nuttiness that lingers on the palate long after you've begun to dream of the next. And even if it were a shadow in comparison to the croissant of my dreams, anything that could satisfy the yearning would be enough. So I began.

My first batches were terrible, indistinguishable from rocks, except for a croissantish shape and color. I tried many variations in the flour, butter, water, and lamination (the ways to layer the butter and dough to create the flaky texture), all of which produced similarly unappetizing results. And to make matters worse, the butter did not cooperate with the dough, or my kitchen was too warm, or the pastries split during proofing, or the dough bounced back too far, making it impossible to roll . . . and a multitude of other errors that I was embarrassed to admit. The building frustration (and a discreetly worried look on my mother's face after she insisted on tasting one) fueled in me an obsessive determination. I spent hours, days, weeks, and months researching everything I could on croissant-making. I pored over threads on forums, read every last bit of literature from textbooks, cookbooks, and flour company newsletters about gluten behavior, proofing, water content in butter, when to layer, how much to layer, when to stop mixing the dough . . . and it went on.

Every source recommended something slightly different, and the only thing I could deduce was that there was no single "right way," considering how different all the variables were, dependent on the country, city, brand of flour, and season. So I was back at the beginning with my only tool, trial and error.

Like a scientist, I began by separating each variable, testing them, tracking every detail in a small black notebook until I happened to hit on something that seemed to work.

At one point, I was sure the butter was the culprit. I knew that the quality at home was certainly inferior to European varieties, so I tested imported, local, and regular butters. I made sure to extract the extra water by hand, squeezing it as some pastry chefs do. (Some even cover their butter with flour and pound it to extract extra moisture.) I had read that making your own butter made a difference, so I decided to try that too.

I drove for hours to a farm across the border that produced unpasteurized cream—I had read that it made better-quality butter—and I researched different DIY churns, contraptions involving screwdrivers and large plastic tubs. I considered buying a churn, but when I pictured myself as a milkmaid I thought better of it. In the end, I tried a food processor method I had read about, and discovered, without a shadow of a doubt, that I, Jackie Kai Ellis, do not make good butter. I accepted this realization quickly, coming away with even less desire to become a milkmaid but with a greater respect for the craft of butter making. I continued to squeeze butter by hand, nearly developing carpal tunnel syndrome but finding that it gave me surprisingly soft skin.

Each test took three days, which meant I was working on three days of doughs before I could see what was wrong with the first batch. So, understandably, when I realized that a batch was a complete failure, I felt sheer annoyance. One day I threw the dough to the ground and walked away. For hours I refused to pick it up, and my defeat, the dough, sat on the floor and grew, unaware of its own smug face. Cleaning it up felt like adding insult to injury, and I was so purely resentful at what felt like a cosmic prank that I gave up.

III

A MONTH LATER, I WAS STRUCK AGAIN WITH A PANG OF desire for a croissant, and it was no use ignoring my sentimentality. I surrendered and picked up my little black notebook to review my past failures, trying to decipher in its code another way of approaching this mystery. I went out and bought a marble slab that fitted the width of my refrigerator exactly, so I could roll on a cool surface. I took every good recipe for a croissant I had, charted out the baker's percentages of each component and started at one extreme, testing each ingredient in 5 percent increments until I reached the other extreme.

Slowly the dough began to feel as I remembered it in Paris: soft yet structured, yielding but still substantial. I began to test different combinations of lamination. There were simple folds, or folding the dough in half; letter folds, folding the dough in thirds; and book folds, which folded the dough into quarters from the outsides in like a book. I tried every possible combination to get the perfect one.

A few more successes and many more failures later, I impatiently waited as my kitchen filled with the warm aromas of yeasty bread and sweet, salty butter melting into itself. The timer sounded, and I opened the oven carefully to peek. I held my breath. Everything seemed to be going well—the croissants seemed to be rising high, the layers were as distinct as I remembered they were in Paris—but I would not allow myself high hopes. I had been tricked before, in this same way. I was wiser.

I allowed the croissants to cool slightly, then cut a few open to inspect the laminations, the crumb, and the profile. I made notes in the little black book, and, finally, I tasted. The crust shattered at the pressure of my mouth, the crumb was chewy and melted, and I tasted mornings in Paris.

THE CROISSANT

This is the recipe we use at Beaucoup Bakery, though I must be quite honest and advise you not to try it unless you are not expecting perfection. Perfection would only be possible with a lot of additional practice, additional research, and a lot of trial and error to adjust the recipe to the ingredients and tools available to you, your weather, and your own technique.

Croissants are so sensitive that even a small variation in a baker's hand can cause a less-than-perfect result. The chefs at Beaucoup train for many months before they hit perfection, and even years later, their croissants can still turn out disappointingly, sometimes without rhyme or reason. A perfect croissant is elusive. There are different styles of viennoiseries: boulanger *(a bread baker's style, which is more rustic and not as refined), and* pâtissier *(a pastry chef's style, which is much more like a fine work of pastry art). My idea of perfection is the latter. In my mind, a perfect croissant must be the color of a stick of cinnamon and be surprisingly light in the hand for its size. It must have defined layers like a fine pleated skirt. The shape must never be curved like a crescent moon or a pair of horns but straight, bulging in the center so it is shaped like a rounded diamond. The reason for this is that in France, curved croissants are those made with margarine and the straight croissant shape indicates that they are made with real butter. In my opinion, only those made of real butter—though it is harder to create the defined layers—are good croissants. The crust should be shatteringly crisp; flakes of it should scatter and fall all over your lap and face.*

When judging the perfect croissant, you must cut it in half vertically along its belly to inspect its cross section. The rounder and higher the shape the better, and the structure on the inside should look like an open network of fine layers resembling a honeycomb. When you eat the croissant, the nuttiness and crispness of the exterior should be paired with

a meltingly soft interior with just enough chew and bounce to satisfy the
parts of us that need bread. The taste should be yeasty, a touch sour
from the days of fermentation that are needed to develop it, and
overwhelmingly buttery but not greasy. You should never need extra
butter with a proper croissant; as with a perfect baguette, nothing else is
needed. If the stars happen to align, and you are lucky enough to discover
a tray of perfect croissants, it's a rush, like a first kiss, the most glorious
feeling of accomplishment and delight that spurs you to try again, and
again. But in reality, on most days we are simply chasing that feeling,
holding our breaths and the memory of it in our minds.

DAY ONE

This recipe will take about 3 days to make from start to finish. It does not require a lot of active time for the first and last day, but it cannot be rushed as the time is what develops the depth of flavor and allows the croissants to rise without overstressing the glutens.

INGREDIENTS FOR THE PRE-FERMENT

I prefer the method of starting the yeast in a pre-ferment because it deepens and develops the flavor of the dough. I have tried other quicker methods but found this to give the best flavor.

100 g flour, divided, T55 or equivalent (see note on flour on page 224)

10 g instant yeast

100 g water at room temperature

In a medium bowl, whisk together 75 g of the flour and the yeast. Add the water and mix well with a spatula until it forms a smooth paste without any lumps. Scrape the sides of the bowl, making sure that all the paste is neatly at the base of the bowl. Dust the remaining 25 g of flour onto the paste, making sure to cover the surface evenly. Allow to rest in a warmish, draft-free room for about 1 hour, until the flour is very cracked on the surface and the pre-ferment has expanded to about double its original size.

450 g flour, T55 or equivalent (see note on flour on page 224)

60 g granulated sugar

14 g fine sea salt

Pre-ferment from above

55 g unsalted butter, 84% milk fat or higher, at room temperature
and cut into small pieces (see note on butter below)

175 g whole milk, 3.5% milk fat, at room temperature

In the bowl of a stand mixer fitted with the dough hook, whisk together the flour, sugar, and salt. Add the pre-ferment and the butter pieces and begin to mix on the lowest setting. Add the milk in a steady stream while mixing, and allow the dough to knead slowly for 6 minutes or until the dough completely comes together into a smoothish ball. When poked, it will feel firm and bounce back slightly. It will feel like moist skin, not sticky or tacky.

Wrap the dough two times in plastic wrap, forming it into a rough 6 × 6-inch square. Allow it to rest at room temperature for 45 minutes to 1 hour. Place it in the freezer for 15 minutes to slow the yeast activity, flipping the dough at 7 minutes to ensure even cooling. Remove the dough from the freezer and place it in the refrigerator overnight until you are ready to laminate the following day.

THE BUTTER PACKAGE

375 g unsalted butter, 84% milk fat or higher,
at slightly colder than room temperature

The intention here is to form a square of butter that is consistent in texture and thickness, and which will eventually be wrapped by the dough in the lamination process described on page 221. In France, butter companies pre-package butter meant for lamination into sheets, which makes it easy to use; however, we have no such thing in North America of the same quality, so my solution was to create the sheets myself.

We are aiming to create a square butter sheet that will be easy to roll into thin sheets between the dough layers. Make sure the butter is pliable but not melted. If it melts, the milk solids and fat will separate, making the structure of the butter inconsistent.

Place the butter on the center of a large piece of parchment paper (about 16 × 16 inches). Flatten it slightly and fold the opposite sides of the parchment together to create a roughly 6 × 6-inch square, being sure to crease the edges to maintain a good square shape.

Once the package of butter is enclosed (it will not seem neat and tidy) use a rolling pin to push the butter to all corners and edges, making a flat sheet of butter about ½ inch thick. Be sure to roll to the edges, eliminating any air pockets, which will create inconsistencies in your croissant. Roll the package to a consistent thickness throughout and place in the refrigerator until you are ready to laminate the following day.

DAY TWO

Lamination is a specific process of repeatedly layering butter and dough to create flaky viennoiseries such as croissants, *pains au chocolat*, *pains aux raisins*, puff pastry, *chaussons aux pommes*, Danishes, *brioches feuilletées*, to name a few. The process is generally the same where a large amount of butter is encased by dough and rolled and folded several times to create layers of butter alternating with dough.

The flakiness is created when the heat from the oven during baking creates steam from the moisture in the butter, causing the dough to rise and expand with pockets. The butter also separates each layer by nature of its oil, and with the rise of the yeast, this all creates the puffy, layered pastry we know as a croissant.

The variations in lamination techniques are numerous. Some prefer to smear the butter into the dough initially, some pound the butter with flour to extract extra moisture and bring the consistency closer to that of the dough, making it easier to roll. Some vary their number of "turns" or how they fold the dough on itself, and still there are variations in working temperature, or where they fold, how they enclose the butter into the dough. There are "letter folds" or "single turns," which is folding the rolled dough into thirds like a letter. There are "book folds" or "double turns," which is when the rolled dough is folded toward the center, 2 times, resembling closing a book twice. Traditionally, croissant consists of 3 "letter folds" making 27 layers of butter and dough. After many tests and variations, I found that 2 book folds worked for me, and 1 book fold and 1 letter fold worked best for my instructors. Some even just fold the dough in half to create an extra "half turn." They all work; it depends on the numerous variances in ingredients, tools, and other environmental factors. It is a fine balancing act, and what's "right," I've discovered, is whatever works best.

The goal of lamination is to get very even layers of butter and dough. This can be done best when the dough and butter are the same consistency and texture so that they roll out at the same rate. If the butter is softer than the dough, the butter will be squeezed out from between the layers of the dough. If the butter is harder than the dough, it begins to separate and crack within the layers like icebergs, and this creates a greasy croissant with imperfect lamination. As different doughs will have different textures, and different butters will melt or be pliable at different temperatures, you must feel the ingredients regularly to monitor their consistency. Generally, the dough needs to be colder than the butter to mimic the texture of a pliable butter. And since the butter cannot be so warm that it melts into the dough, generally the dough must adjust to the butter.

This recipe was perfected using a dough sheeter, a commercial machine that rolls the dough evenly and quickly, allowing the dough and butter to maintain their temperatures during lamination. Rolling by hand is not impossible but will require you to place the dough in the refrigerator to cool for a few minutes, until it is just cold enough to roll without melting the butter into the dough but not so cold that the butter becomes harder than the dough. If rolling by hand, it needs to be done fast enough that the dough doesn't begin to proof, or the air bubbles will cause the lamination to be disrupted.

LAMINATION AND ROLLING

1 butter package (as described on page 219)

1 dough package from Day One

Flour for dusting

Take the butter package out to temper it to the consistency of cold dough. You can re-roll the butter package to make it pliable and consistent because when it is tempering, often the edges are warmer than the center.

Remove the dough from the refrigerator, and on a lightly floured surface, roll the dough into a 6 × 13-inch rectangle, always rolling as square as possible so the wastage is decreased. Place the butter in the center of the dough and wrap the dough around the butter. Pinch the dough to seal the butter in, making sure to eliminate any air bubbles or excess flour.

When rolling the dough, you must remember to alternate the direction with each turn. Since the dough is being rolled and stretched longer in one direction with each turn, it must be rolled in the other direction the following time or the dough will be stretched too far in one direction, making it impossible to roll as well as weakening the gluten structure. For example, if the dough was just rolled to 6 × 13 inches, the following roll should elongate the 6-inch length.

Roll the dough to 24 × 7 inches (the pinched ends should be the short side this time) in as straight a rectangle as possible. Cut 1–2 inches off each end to eliminate the excess dough that does not contain any butter sandwiched between it. Make a book fold, wrap in plastic, and let rest in the refrigerator to relax the glutens, but not so long that the butter hardens too much, 10–15 minutes.

Repeat the last step, making sure the open ends become the short end this turn and resting again in the refrigerator.

The rolling for this step tends to be a bit tricky by hand and will require you to place the dough in and out of the refrigerator to keep relaxing the glutens until you can roll the dough to the desired thickness. Roll out the dough to 13 × 15 inches, 3.5–4.5 mm thick, and cut the edges so that the true layer of lamination can be free to expand.

To cut your croissant into triangle shapes, begin to measure intervals of 3 inches along the longer side of the dough and make small cuts to indicate the intervals. Along the opposite side, measure 1.5 inches inward from the edge and make small cuts to indicate intervals of 3 inches. Using a long, sharp knife, cut from marker to marker on the opposite sides in a zigzag pattern, to create long triangles of dough.

Once the triangles are cut, use your fingers to lightly stretch the triangle lengthwise and then roll tightly from the wide end to the thin point, ensuring that it is evenly centered. If not, the croissant will proof lopsided. Place the croissant on a sheet tray lined with parchment paper with the "tail" of the croissant tucked under its belly.

Repeat with the remaining triangles, wrap in plastic, and place in the refrigerator overnight to begin cold proofing.

PROOFING

Remove the croissants from the refrigerator and arrange them on sheet trays lined with parchment paper with 3–5 inches of space between them. Allow them to sit at room temperature, in the shade and covered lightly with plastic wrap for 4–7 hours (depending on the ambient temperature), or until the croissants have doubled to tripled in size and they look like wobbly pillows.

BAKING

EGG WASH

1 egg

1 tbsp whipping cream

½ tsp fine sea salt

In a small bowl, gently whisk all the ingredients together.

Preheat the oven to 425°F.

Using a pastry brush, gently brush the egg wash onto the tops of the proofed croissants.

Place the croissants in the oven and bake for 7 minutes. Without opening the oven, reduce the temperature to 375°F and bake for another 7 minutes. Turn the trays at this point and bake for a further 5 minutes, or until the outsides are golden brown. If you have a convection oven, turn off the fan, or the crust will be too dry.

Allow the croissants to cool on the trays until they are warm enough to touch. Cut one open to inspect your lamination and taste the flavor development.

Serve warm or at room temperature.

A NOTE ON THE MEASUREMENTS: As with most professional recipes, the measurements in this recipe are indicated in weight, which is much more precise than volume. Everyone has a different way of measuring; some people tend to pack an ingredient into a cup, whereas others will lightly sprinkle it in. This creates a large variance in the amount of the actual ingredient added. For example, one cup of flour measured by one person could weigh over 0.5 oz (more or less) than when measured by another. With croissants, if the balance of the recipe is changed, it can also drastically change your final results. Using weight measurements ensures consistency and accuracy.

A NOTE ON FLOUR: I have specified an equivalent to a T55 flour. T55 is a type of French flour that performs most like an all-purpose flour in North America, though all-purpose flours all over the world are extremely varied and behave vastly differently. What a French T55 can do is be both elastic and durable at once. The glutens in this flour are much like a strong elastic band that can be stretched easily but doesn't break. Many strong flours in Canada are like strong but brittle bands that tear easily when they are stretched, making it difficult to roll the layers thin. On the other hand, the softer flours don't have any elasticity at all, making it impossible to hold the air the dough needs to rise. A firmer dough will create a flakier product, though the firmer the dough, the more risk there is that it will tear, which is why some add a good amount of butter to it to add suppleness.

Over the course of developing my croissant recipe, I created a proprietary blend of commercial flours to mimic the ones I had worked with in France. Depending on where you are in the world, you will be able to source different flours and, unfortunately, they will all behave differently than mine. So this is where you must do a bit of testing on your own to find a type of flour that works best.

A NOTE ON BUTTER: Croissants require a high-quality butter with a percentage of milk fat of 84% or higher. The goal is to roll the butter into thin sheets alternating with layers of dough, so the more pliable it is, the easier it will be to achieve that result. Having less moisture in the butter, leaving more fat, will make the texture more pliable, more similar to the texture of the dough, at a colder temperature and is thus less prone to melting. The higher milk fat butter is also firmer at room temperature than regular butter, which also aids in keeping the right texture for lamination.

The moisture level alone doesn't dictate how pliable a butter is when it is cold. Churning butter is a specialized craft in France. You have a multitude of choices in grocery stores and in cheese shops (*doux, salé, demi-sel*, from different regions, raw milk, pasteurized) and the ones that are well made can be spread onto toast right out of the fridge. The way you can tell it is pliable when it is cold is to poke or squeeze it. Does it give a little, or does it feel like a block of unforgiving ice? Usually French butters with higher moisture will be more pliable at a cold temperature than a Canadian butter with less moisture because they are made with more expertise.

A NOTE ABOUT THE CHAPTER: Indeed, the process of creating the croissant was arduous for me, probably more so than if I had been a more seasoned chef. Regardless, where this chapter ends was only halfway through the process. So as not to make the reader suffer as thoroughly as I did at the time, I omitted many more failures. And again, I think it would be fair to mention that we still cannot create a perfect croissant each time; it's precisely why we love and hate the croissant so much. The perfect croissant is rare, so when it comes, we appreciate it that much more.

MAKES 7–9 CROISSANTS, depending on how much extra dough is cut and how thin you are able to roll it. I scaled this recipe to fit comfortably into a KitchenAid mixer, and it can be comfortably rolled out on a small countertop.

LETTING GO

$\{2011-2014\}$

YOU COULD NOT STEP TWICE

INTO THE SAME RIVER,

FOR IT'S NOT THE *same river*

AND YOU'RE NOT

THE SAME MAN.

Heraclitus

THROUGHOUT MY LIFE, I'VE FELT POWER IN WATER. SOME
people and cultures say it has magical properties or ancient
knowledge hidden in its substance, and I tend to agree.

From a very young age I've held a reverence for it, as well as a
fear. When I was four years old, I tried to learn how to swim, but
I refused to put my head under the water, knowing even then that
it had the ability to drown me. An awe-infused uneasiness over-
comes me when I look out at vast seas stretching so far that they
meet the edge of the earth. Standing feebly near crashing seas on
windy days stirs me to imagine the force of a tidal wave on my
body, and I often feel a need to cross faraway oceans, or I feel a
landlocked longing for familiar shores when I'm searching for
something or missing someone from the past.

We drink when we feel thirsty, and are refreshed. But of all
the magic that water holds, I've discovered that sometimes a long,
hot shower is the best medicine.

I

(2012)

I AM IN A WIDE, RAPID RIVER, TURBULENT IN PATCHES where it tumbles and skips around rocks peeking over its surface, with calmer streams snaking between. The river is forceful, rushing me toward the unknown. I feel afraid. I use every minute muscle, every movement, to swim against the current, but I am still being pulled downstream. Futile . . .

That image poured into my mind as my body shook, my stomach clenching and unclenching rhythmically, independently, alien. I was sitting on the floor of my living room. It was warm but my body disagreed, and I felt cold. I tried to get up for a blanket but I couldn't move and my legs trembled weakly. There was a cold tingling and aching in my eardrums that caused every sound but the one of my heavy breathing to be muffled. I was having a panic attack. Unsure of what else to do, I held myself, waiting for it to pass.

Why was this happening? I scanned my life. I was in the midst of starting a bakery, something I had no idea how to do. I was smart enough to know that. Meticulously researching statistics on all the potential failures, I made note of them all. Only one in eleven bakeries survive past the first year. Some don't even make it to opening before they go bankrupt due to unexpected expenses. As the owner, I fully expected to give up traveling, as I heard that I would most likely be tied to the business. As much as I love seeing the world, I was willing to give that up in order for my Beaucoup dream to be realized. I heard that holidays would be overcome by the bakery's needs, and so Thanksgivings and Christmases, my favorite times of year, would never be the same again. But I was willing to give that up too. I had carefully weighed each pro and con, and in the end, I concluded that I would regret it for the rest of my life if I didn't try opening the bakery, even if I failed. So I jumped in.

It was something about architects, general contractors, mechanical engineers, and equipment suppliers that tipped me over the edge. It was hard to know whom to trust on topics I knew nothing of, what the "right" thing to do was. I was worried I was going to be taken advantage of, which would cause some catastrophic chain of events. I was worried I was going to fail, my mind swimming constantly with thoughts of everything that could go "wrong." I was exhausted and frightened, and I simply couldn't keep up with everything I couldn't control.

. . . *My body is drained, and I stop swimming. I sink into the water and my head stays afloat. When I regain my breath, I can feel the water flowing around me, carrying me gently. I look downstream and can see a few miles of patches of turbulence and calm. I discover that the river propels me as I move from one side to the other, helping me toward patches I want to explore and away from ones I want to avoid. Surprisingly, it feels effortless, a letting go, and I close my eyes.*

My body was calm. I began to warm up. I had clarity that everyone choosing to live was in a river too. There was no controlling the direction that it flowed or what came next. I saw the vanity in swimming against the current, as if I could control nature itself. And I was given an opportunity to explore the water, comfortably submerged within it.

In that moment, I learned to trust life.

I I

(2011)

WE WALKED ALONG THE NETWORK OF SHALLOW RIVERS springing to and from Havasu Falls in Arizona. The water flowed, covering just the tops of our feet. At its deepest, we could wade up to our waists, gripping crevices in the river rock with our feet to keep the gentle current from tipping us over.

The day before we had hiked a few hours down into the Grand Canyon, into the Havasupai Reservation, and the plan was to camp at the base for a few days. The canyon was a beautiful maze of red rock and emerald waters, forming little pools, dramatic waterfalls, and caves just wide enough for us to crawl through. We descended further, clinging to old rope ladders and metal bars that had been drilled into stone walls forty feet high, and for whatever reason, fear was suspended in the entire canyon, and we explored without inhibition.

We came up to a thirty-foot waterfall that dropped into a tiny pool so deep that I could only see darker shades of greens and blues the farther down my eyes tried to focus. One by one, the eight men I was camping with dove, falling alongside the water and into the blue. There was shouting, cheering, laughing, then quiet for a small moment before they emerged with water still clinging to their faces. They swam to the small copper-colored shore to wait for the others.

I never learned to swim, so I climbed down the side of the falls to the lowest edge of the water, three feet from the surface. I watched the divers, envious, wanting so badly to feel water on my body. But when I looked into it, searching for a bottom, I found nothing to support my sinking weight. So I sat as each of the men hiked back to the top to plummet once again.

My yearning intensified until it overcame my fear and I shouted, "I'm going to jump in."

"Are you sure?" yelled one of the guys, brows furrowed.

"Yes. How can I possibly drown with eight of you watching me?" I yelled back, fighting my fear with logic.

I stood at the edge of the water, looking into nothingness. I hesitated. I wanted to turn back and unmake a fervent decision, but I knew this chance may never come again. So I took a deep breath and jumped.

The water was just as deeply turquoise from below as it was from above. I heard no shouting, cheering, or laughing, only the sound of moving water on my eardrums. I saw light above me and moved my way toward it with flailing limbs, mimicking swimming movements. I came up, gasping for air in dead silence. I struggled to shore, as if moving through watery quicksand, and grasped the first rock I saw. I looked up to see every single body poised to rescue me, and when I smiled, they cheered.

In that moment, I learned to be brave.

III

(2014)

I WAS IN A HAPPY, BUBBLING RIVER, AND THERE I SAT heavy in the center of it, with my body wedged between two large boulders. My eyes were gazing downstream, watching where the sunlight danced and shimmered on the surface. I suddenly felt the gravity of the moment.

For months I was confused, unsure. It came on slowly and I didn't notice it right away, but something didn't feel right to me. I described this vague sense of discontent and confusion to my best friend D. And after taking in all my hazy confusion, he asked me a question, so pure and uncomplicated: "What do you want?"

"I want to travel," I replied immediately, surprising myself with my own clarity.

"OK, well, see you later!" he smiled, waving farewell.

That night I booked a flight. I wanted to go back to a place where I could remember hearing my own voice so clearly. I'm not sure how else to describe it other than that it was like having a conversation with the most sacred part of me. So I packed my bags, left everything in Vancouver, including the bakery, rented a car, and drove with clarity as a mission.

I started with a long hike and sat in a river, feeling the current rock me gently and watching the light sparkle through the trees onto the currents. I held in my hand some dried leaves, a symbol of everything I knew I needed to let go of. G and I had divorced years earlier, but memories of him and our marriage were still lodged in me, not always in the obvious ways I expected. I didn't long for him or have regrets; I guess I expected that letting go would be like finishing a novel you were reading. But letting go turned out to be much more like rereading a poem over time, and seeing different meanings within the words, separate and combined.

I put out my arm, my fingers holding the memories of G and our marriage, and when they unfolded, the river washed the leaves, and the memories, away. I grasped for them again instinctively, because in some ways they were comforting, but they had drifted too far, so I let them go once again.

I climbed the same hilltop I had climbed years before and, perched on a rock, I explained to myself, "Look, I have a week, and in this time I need some clarity on what to do." I had also been grappling with some seemingly larger decisions that loomed in my mind as the culprits for my mental fog. Should I leave my lover? Should I be doing what I'm doing now? What do I want to do next? What makes me happy?

And I answered myself, "Just relax and enjoy. Everything will still be waiting for you a week from now. Today, do whatever brings you joy, because if you know what gives you joy today, tomorrow will eventually become today and you will have your answers."

So in that moment, I learned again to trust life.

EGGS

{1986–2011}

I LOVE EGGS FRIED *over* MEDIUM.

Slick Rick

EGGS ARE WONDERFUL THINGS. IN COOKING, THEY ARE stabilizers, clarifiers, retarders, emulsifiers, binders, leaveners, among other things. They add color, flavor, and numerous textures. And let's face it: among the most comforting things to eat are fluffy scrambled eggs on hot buttered toast.

I

AT THE AGE OF SEVEN, ONE IS USUALLY OLD ENOUGH TO know how they like their eggs. My uncle asked me how I wanted them cooked for breakfast, and I ran through the options in my mind, deliberately choosing the one that made my mouth water at the thought of it: sunny-side up.

When I arrived at the table, there sat in front of me a curly mass of eggs, scrambled, beside my toast. I rarely complained or spoke up, knowing it wasn't the place of a small child, but surely this was a mistake. Perhaps someone else was eating my eggs? Maybe my uncle misheard?

I looked at my plate and said simply, "But I said sunny-side up." Everyone began to chuckle, reminding me that this wasn't a restaurant and that it was easier to make scrambled for everyone.

Why had they even bothered to ask if they had no intention of fulfilling the request? What kind of games were they playing with me?! I had imagined dipping my toast into the yolk, and then placing the rest of the white on top of the second slice with a good amount of butter and salt. I began crying at the table, at the cruelty of it.

II

MY FAVORITE PASTRY AS A CHILD WAS A CHINESE EGG tart. I ate them methodically, taking a small spoon and scooping out the custardy insides, scraping the pastry clean. And then I would split the pastry with my spoon and enjoy each flaky bite until it was gone.

III

G AND I WERE AT A BISTRO IN THE 11TH ARRONDISSEMENT. The meal was relatively forgettable, but the dessert, *îles flottantes*, oh! The experience is still imprinted on the most important parts of my brain, never again to be replicated or relived. This is usually the case with the best of them.

It was a square, not a mound, of ethereal white meringue, bathing in a shallow bowl of cold *crème anglaise* sprinkled with a small handful of caramelized sliced almonds and topped with a generous drizzle of tawny caramel. The soft whites disappeared on my tongue like suds in a bath, and when I ate it with a spoon-ful of cold, heavy, sweet custard, it felt simply . . . luxurious.

IV

IN PASTRY SCHOOL ONE OF THE BASICS I LEARNED WAS that of *traiteur*, catered foods. One of the dishes was a gently cooked, coddled egg, *oeufs en cocotte*. It was slowly cooked until the egg began to thicken and come together. I mixed slowly, making sure that no bit of egg ever felt the warmth for long, and eventually the entire mass became just like thick pudding. It didn't seem like much in the pan or on a plate, but then I topped it with *fines herbes* and dipped *bâtons* of toast into the center. It was velvety and it made up for the transgressions of that moment at the breakfast table when I was seven.

SCRAMBLED EGGS ON HOT BUTTERED TOAST

*This is how I make my scrambled eggs. It's how my grandmother
and mother made them; I think it is how scrambled eggs
are made in Hong Kong, where my mom grew up.*

2 large eggs, with the yellowest yolks,
from the happiest birds you can find or afford

2 tbsp whipping cream

¼ tsp fine sea salt

⅛ tsp freshly cracked pepper

1 slice of good bread

2 tbsp unsalted butter, divided

Crack the eggs into a medium bowl, omitting any shell. Using chopsticks in a whisking motion, incorporate the cream, salt, and pepper until the mixture is smooth and homogeneous.

Heat a nonstick pan over high heat. In the meantime, toast the slice of bread. When the pan is hot, drop in 1 tablespoon of butter and allow it to melt and foam slightly, swirling it to coat the bottom of the pan.

Pour in the egg mixture and let it sit for a few seconds, until you can see the edges begin to bubble away from the pan. This means that it has created a thin layer of cooked egg on the bottom of the pan. Tilt and swirl the pan slightly so that the uncooked egg pours into the empty space. Use the chopsticks to push the silky curds to one side of the pan, and swirl the remaining uncooked egg to the empty side of the pan. Continue this process until the eggs are about 75%–85% cooked and still runny on top, and then remove them from the heat. Transfer the eggs immediately to a warm plate to stop the cooking.

Spread the remaining 1 tablespoon of butter on the hot toast so that it melts into the bread. Place a bite of scrambled egg on the toast using a fork and take a bite. Stop. Enjoy. Continue this process until both the egg and toast are eaten.

MAKES 1 SERVING.

HOW TO OPEN A FINANCIALLY
SUCCESSFUL BAKERY

{2012}

"WHAT ARE WE?"

ISABELLE ASKED ISAAC ONE NIGHT, CURIOUS ...

"I THINK,"

HE SAID CONTEMPLATIVELY INTO THE DARK,

"WE ARE EACH *a chair and a ladder*

FOR THE OTHER."

Erica Bauermeister, The School
of Essential Ingredients

IN THE MONTHS BEFORE G MOVED OUT, I WAS RESEARCHING how to open a bakery. I started with a very apropos book, called *How to Open a Financially Successful Bakery.* When I told an acquaintance of it, he laughed at me. He was a Harvard MBA grad, and though I wasn't, I could see the obvious humor in the situation. The reality was that I had never worked in the food industry at all, let alone opened a bakery. I had no idea where to start, and the best people to ask—bakery owners—were understandably not always willing to share information. So I started with the book, carefully reading it to prime myself with as much information as possible.

I

THE QUESTION "WHAT DO YOU WANT TO DO?" IS A DOUBLE-edged, privileged one. As a child, I was often reminded that having a choice was a gift. My mother grew up very poor, in the shanty-towns of Hong Kong. She had wanted so desperately to be educated, to be a doctor, and she could easily have been one if she had had the luxury.

I grew up hearing stories about how she was beaten by school-teachers for wearing a uniform that was too short. I guess they thought she was trying to be scandalous, but in reality, it was because she didn't have the money for a new one, and children grow tall so quickly. She told me about how she did well in school, always placing second in her class until she was forced to quit so that she could work in factories to earn money for her large family. She was one of the older children but still so young that she had to borrow fake identification in order to work at all. And in the same breath, she would tell me that the best student in her class eventually became a surgeon, all the while reading my encyclopedias from front to back in the night after we had all gone to sleep, and repeating facts about Austria or zygotes the following day.

So while I felt lucky to have had opportunities in life that my mom never did, for many earlier years having a choice was mixed with guilt. And no matter how lucky one is or isn't, questions always feel heavy and full of anxiety, and the longer they stay precariously in the air without the relief of answers, the more they tire you out.

I I

WHEN I WAS FOUR, I WANTED TO BE SPIDERMAN. IT seemed like the perfect career: adventurous, fulfilling, I could help people, it afforded a unique means of transportation, and if that were not enough, I could wear a cool red outfit, a genuine perk to me at any age. My dream ended when my sister told me I couldn't be Spiderman because I wasn't a man, and there was a "man" in the name. So instead of arguing with that logic, I decided to be a fashion designer instead. This was my career goal until I was sixteen, when I failed sewing class over a small misunderstanding—I guess I couldn't just chat in class and sew at home. The ability to pass a sewing class seemed like a required skill to be a fashion designer, like a web-making class would be to a career as Spiderman.

As with my sewing failure, as with the ending of art school, design school, and now pastry school, I was once again deciding what to do with my life. I'd had jobs and careers, developed talents and skills, made money, found security—but something was always missing. The accolades had a sheen that wore off soon after they had arrived. I needed my work, how I spent my days, to mean something to me. I needed to know I was doing something that satisfied the deepest cravings in me to express those innate and creative parts of myself that were unique to the way I saw the world. But I also needed to know I was making something better outside of me, out in the world, even if it was minuscule and no one was better off but me and a handful of other people.

I think I've always needed that, to do something I believed in, with a greater purpose. I'm not sure if it's something we choose, and I'm not sure why I hurt for it so much, but all I can say is that, without it, it always feels like I'm sitting in a waiting room, entertaining myself pointlessly, biding time until . . . who knows what.

If I stop to think of all the people I've known—family, friends, lovers, people I thought I knew from lives I filled in with my imagination—I've met some with the same desperate longing and some without. But I do believe everyone does, in some way or another, want purpose; to know that every hardship is for something bigger than themselves.

Or maybe this I've imagined, too.

III

FROM THE MOMENT I HAD MET HER, G'S MOTHER WOULD
give me books each Christmas and birthday. Some were cookbooks, because she knew how much I loved them, and some were
books on food because I loved those, too. She read extensively herself, and I always appreciated that she understood, perhaps more
than I, the private beauty created by words picked carefully and
then arranged side by side.

Two years before I went to pastry school in Paris, she gave
me a novel about a woman with a restaurant where she taught
cooking classes. In the story, food (her food) wove its way through
her students' lives and healed them. And in turn, she was also
healed through those that she taught, connecting to her own past
and to herself.

There was a moment in the book that clung to me. A woman
asks her lover what they are to each other, and he replies, "ladders and chairs." There was something in that that I immediately
loved: being a place to climb if the one you love was in need of
inspiration, or a place to rest, should he or she need that instead.
It reminded me of my Saturday mornings, and of what food
meant to me.

After I returned from Paris and I began planning the opening
of Beaucoup, it wasn't enough for me just to open a bakery. I needed
to create something that had a chance of making a difference to
people, and to me, even if it was a seemingly insignificant one.

The vision and the desire for Beaucoup came so naturally
that it felt like breathing, as if it had been written on me word by
word, slowly over time. I wanted to do for others what bakeries
and cafés had done for me during the years when I felt confused
and even afterward, when I started to feel sure of myself and

about the world I was in. I wanted it to be a "ladder or chair" for someone, to give the same gift of rest and inspiration that food had given me. I wanted to create Saturday mornings—a book, a coffee, a double-baked almond croissant—for others, out of gratitude for the Saturday mornings that helped me reclaim my life. So I built Beaucoup holding that firmly in my mind.

IV

MAGNETIC . . . OR MAYBE LOVE? IT'S THE ONLY WAY I can describe that rare intersection of passion, purpose, talents being challenged, and honest-to-goodness hard work. I couldn't help but be immersed in my passion, surrounded by the presence of it, and fall into it with my whole being. Beaucoup was all I wanted, though I didn't have any idea what I was doing.

But I did know how to research, and I became an expert in Googling, starting with the search, "how to start a bakery." So there on the internet I researched everything from demographics and market research to what to look for in a lease, places to lease, how to apply for grants, how to write a business plan, how to apply for a loan, point of sale systems, coffee machines, and operations plans—to name a few topics. I went to government business resources to ask for legal, accounting, and importing advice, I joined business groups and forums to ask questions. I looked for months for the right place to rent, consulting the clerks at the city about bylaws and requirements. Since I was a total novice, I was thankful that so many people were willing to teach me and point me in the right direction. I was diligent, knowing that my inexperience was enough of a disadvantage that I needed to be even more thorough to compensate. I even cold-called businesses to see if they would give me thirty minutes to interview them with carefully drafted questions on everything I didn't know, and then everything I didn't know I didn't know.

In the course of my planning, I began to meet like-minded food entrepreneurs—artisanal ice cream producers, craft doughnut shops, custom cake makers—in the same boat, just starting out, figuring it out together, all with a passion for food and for creating beautiful-tasting things. We all shared a commissary space that I rented as I was testing the last stages of my croissant recipe on commercial equipment.

One day, for fun, I baked a sour cherry pie from local cherries that I found at the market. I made a flaky crust with duck fat, imagining the savory flavor contrasted with the tart and sweet filling. We all gathered around, my new food friends and I, added dollops of a bright cardamom ice cream that another person had made, and moaned with pleasure from the combination of the melting crust with the slight hint of almond in the cherries and the fragrant creaminess of the cardamom embracing it all on our palates. On other days, my friend M and I drizzled a salted caramel sauce that he had made over my test croissants (and anything else we could find). We ate so many it made us feel like we'd committed naughty deeds.

I was part of a true community. When one of us needed advice on a flavor or when a texture wasn't coming out quite right, we would all gather and brainstorm solutions. We helped and encouraged each other because we knew that though we were small, we were stronger together. We did it out of gratitude for the times we were given help and for a passion to see the others like us succeed. Maybe it gave us hope that we could too. But most of all, we did it because it was just plain fun, like playing with friends who loved the same game. I loved food, and for the first time since childhood, I was surrounded by people who truly understood and would find it quite normal to drive to a different city for a good taco or wax on about the many possible uses for grains of paradise.

It was after dozens and dozens of tests and failures at the commissary kitchen that, one day, I finally perfected my croissant. There had been so many failed tests that I was beginning to doubt the possibility of the perfect croissant. And unfortunately, since croissants required such specific knowledge, which none of my friends had, they were at a loss to help me.

That day, after hours in the kitchen, I opened the finicky oven and there they were, exactly as I remembered them in Paris: toasted, golden puffs of yeasty butter. I passed the warm croissants around to the chefs and aspiring entrepreneurs around me, and watched as they melted into pools where they stood, in disbelief that such a croissant existed in the world. I felt as if I had transported these croissants from Paris, and I felt so extremely proud to know that I'd made some people very happy that day.

SALTED CARAMEL SAUCE FOR REALLY ANYTHING

This caramel thickens up drastically as it cools in the fridge. You can use it chilled and thick, spread on brioches like a pâte à tartiner, *or warmed slightly to be thinner and drizzled over croissants, as M and I did.*

¾ cup (5.5 oz/160 g) granulated sugar

1 vanilla bean, sliced lengthwise and scraped
of its seeds and husk reserved

⅔ cup (5.5 oz/160 g) whipping cream (35% milk fat), warmed

½ cup (4.5 oz/125 g) unsalted butter

⅛ tsp (0.4 g) fine sea salt

Place the sugar and vanilla bean seeds and husk into a medium-large pot. Melt and caramelize the sugar over medium-high heat, swirling the pan constantly to evenly melt the sugar. The sugar will be ready when it reaches a deep amber color (216°F–217°F if tested with a candy thermometer).

Wear an oven mitt, then take the sugar off the heat and carefully pour in the warmed cream and salt. The mixture will bubble vigorously and the steam will be very hot, so be careful.

When the bubbling subsides, stir the caramel with a wooden spoon until well mixed. The caramelized sugar will be stiff at first, but will melt slowly into the cream as you continue to stir it. If necessary, put the pot back onto low heat and reheat to fully dissolve. Add the butter and stir until it is all melted and emulsified.

Allow the caramel to cool to room temperature and remove the vanilla husk. Keep refrigerated until ready to use. This can be stored in the refrigerator for up to 2 weeks.

A NOTE ON THE MEASUREMENTS: This recipe is commonly seen in both weight and volume measurements, but I've done my version in volume as the proportions in caramel sauce can be more flexible than other pastry recipes. A thermometer would be extremely helpful in gauging when the sugar is done caramelizing.

MAKES 1½ CUPS.

LETTING GO

{2012}

AND THE DAY CAME

WHEN THE RISK TO *remain tight in a bud*

WAS MORE PAINFUL

THAN THE RISK IT TOOK

to blossom.

Anaïs Nin

"IT'S A WEEK UNTIL AUGUST 23. SHALL WE SET A TIME to talk?"

My heart pounded, and my voice faltered almost imperceptibly, but I assumed he caught it. I had waited for this day for nearly six months.

"Yeah, sure. Should we say after dinner that day?" G said it so casually that, to an outsider, we could have been meeting about which shower curtains to order online, or something equally ordinary, like whether to host a Mexican night or a stuff-your-own-baked-potato party.

"OK. Sounds good," I replied.

While sitting on the couch during one of our Monday meetings six months earlier, I had told him one day, matter-of-factly, as a simple acknowledgment of reality, "I want to let you know that I feel like I've done everything I can think of, and I think we should consider a divorce," I said.

"I don't think so." I was thrown off by the conviction in his voice. It seemed mismatched with the repetitive tone of our other conversations.

"OK. I'm willing to try anything you suggest. Let me know. I just have to tell you that I'm done thinking of ideas, and I have nothing left." A small part of me revived and wanted to honor his intention, to give it one more shot, to stand up once more for us, but it collapsed just as suddenly.

"I don't think it's done."

"I know. Well, I'm open to any suggestions, just let me know what you want to try."

Over the next six months, nothing happened. We didn't fight anymore. In my mind, there was nothing to save, nothing to fight for. G and I just coexisted.

I waited for him to join me where I was, acceptance.

On August 23 we met. We sat on the bed in his room and didn't bother with pleasantries. We both knew why we were meeting, and pleasantries were all we had exchanged for months now anyway.

"So, can you admit that it's not working anymore?" I asked gently. I think we both knew that what I was really asking was, "Can you let me go now?"

"Yes."

So it was done. We spent the following weeks ironing out the practical details of tearing our lives apart, with as much love and respect as we could find in the remains.

Seven years before, I had vowed to love him for the rest of my life, and I intended to keep my promise. Only it wouldn't be through living with him day after day, or experiencing life beside him. I wouldn't love him as his wife, but as me.

MEXICAN WEDDING COOKIES

These cookies were G's favorite. Even today, he still asks me about them.
And when I am feeling grateful for the experiences we shared and
what I've learned from them, I bake some for him.

2 cups (8.8 oz/250 g) all-purpose flour

1½ cups (6 oz/170 g) toasted and cooled pecans, coarsely ground

2 cups (8 oz/227 g) confectioner's sugar, divided

¼ tsp fine sea salt

2 sticks (8 oz/227 g) unsalted butter, room temperature

2 tsp (10 ml) vanilla extract (I prefer Nielsen-Massey)

1½ tsp (7.5 ml) cinnamon

Whisk the flour, pecans, ½ cup of confectioner's sugar, and salt together in a large bowl or the bowl of a stand mixer. Add the butter and mix until it comes together into a consistent dough. Add the vanilla extract and mix again until just incorporated. Cover the bowl with plastic wrap and refrigerate for 30 minutes to let the dough stiffen slightly. This will make it easier to roll into balls.

Preheat the oven to 350°F.

Whisk the cinnamon and remainder of the confectioner's sugar in a large bowl. When the dough is chilled, scoop out and roll balls about 1 inch in diameter (or use a small #45—¾ fluid ounce—ice cream scoop) onto the parchment-paper-lined sheet pan about 1 inch apart.

Bake the cookies for 15–20 minutes or until the edges are caramelized and medium golden brown. Cool them for about 15 minutes and then toss each one in the bowl of spiced sugar. Place the coated cookies on a rack to cool completely. Toss the cookies in the sugar again and serve. Can be stored in an airtight container for up to 3 days.

A NOTE ON THE MEASUREMENTS: I've left both weight and volume measurements here. This is a recipe for the home baker, but I bake in weight and find it easier, so I thought I would give you both.

A NOTE ON THE CINNAMON SUGAR: If you have leftover sugar, you can save it for the next batch of cookies or add it to whipped cream to make cinnamon whipped cream.

MAKES ABOUT 36 COOKIES.

HOW TO OPEN A FINANCIALLY
SUCCESSFUL BAKERY

{2013}

ALL EXTREMES *of* FEELING

are ALLIED *to* MADNESS.

Virginia Woolf, Orlando

I'VE HEARD THIS THOUGHT ECHOED BY OTHER RESTAURATEURS and entrepreneurs: had they known what lay ahead, they would have chosen not to begin at all. And there are instances where being ignorant is quite helpful and instances where it can be quite harmful. With Beaucoup, I recognize that I was incredibly lucky, but my ignorance was indeed both.

I

THE NIGHT BEFORE I OPENED BEAUCOUP, I WAS WRITING an inspirational quote on the chalk wall and someone asked me if I was anxious. If I was worried that people wouldn't like the pastries, or wouldn't like what I had created. That it seemed as if there was so much anticipation built up that most likely I would disappoint. But I felt strangely calm and replied simply, "I've done everything I can. I can't please everyone. I'm proud of what we've done, and the rest is not in my control."

The next morning, I was shocked to see a line forming outside. Everyone was smiling and eager. When I went to open the door, there was no ceremonious pause, no acknowledgment that this moment would become so significant, changing my life in ways I could not have foreseen. I just unlocked the door.

11

I DID TRY TO UNDERSTAND, AS MUCH AS I COULD, THE risks and sacrifices that would come with starting a business. I knew that most start-up business owners don't make any income for the first three years. So I moved out of the home I owned and rented a tiny, dark basement apartment with electrical wires hanging from the ceiling and mouse droppings hidden in the cupboards. It cost half what I rented mine out for, and I planned to live off the difference. I bought a blow-up mattress in case the situation got so dire that I needed to move into the bakery's loft and asked the bakery's landlord if I could use the shower on the second floor of the building if I ever needed it. It was an extreme change, but I didn't care about any of it. I just wanted to see it happen, this dream of mine, and I was willing to do anything to see it succeed.

In the midst of the construction and planning, I sold at farmers' markets, catered events, hosted preopening neighborhood parties, and used every means of getting our name out there. I talked to everyone I met about the bakery: strangers in line at the grocery store, my bank tellers, those in the food community, and people I knew through social media. I radiated pride and passion for my bakery in everything I did, and it created a buzz very naturally. But even so, I simply didn't know what to expect—certainly not the instantaneous demand that happened when I opened, like a flash flood.

From the first day, it felt like a maddened frenzy, with line-ups and media visits, interviews, and TV appearances, and we were selling out before the day was half over. Since the opening of the bakery had been so delayed due to construction and permitting, I had done everything I could to keep the momentum, and had unknowingly built it to a speed I didn't expect.

I thought about the business plan I had written about a year before the bakery opened. I had expected about fifty people a day and had created backup plans for slower weekday afternoons— baking classes for kids, standing on the street wearing a sandwich board and handing out flyers to draw people into my smaller side street. I had planned to hire two people, one to help me in the kitchen in the afternoons, and another to help in the front when I was busy baking in the morning. I had dreams of knowing every one of my customers by name, memorizing their birthdays and their children's birthdays, so that on those days I would give them a cookie or their usual coffee on the house. I also expected never to travel, to celebrate every holiday in the kitchen, essentially, to live at my bakery, tied to the ovens. And the thought made me happy, alongside the idea that I would be a part of a small community of people that found a home in a place I created. I wanted my food to remind them of the comfort and happiness I had found in food in the years before.

By the time we opened our doors, the situation had changed drastically and I adapted. There was now a team of twenty, with over 500 people coming a day, and not a second to be slow. Everyone asked me why I had opened such a small space, disappointed that we couldn't produce more from our tiny kitchen and that there were never seats in the café. But as much as I had prepared for the worst, I had never imagined a scenario like this. So I just did what I could, working around the clock and making a lot of mistakes. I was trying to learn as quickly as I could about what I was supposed to be doing.

I started the business on my own, but help came from every direction, and people multiplied out of nowhere. Friends, family, industry, my own team: they all came like a steady march of relief, a lineup of firefighters controlling the blaze. My mom and dad showed up in the wee hours of the night, when the bakery was closed, to help me wash floors. I was worrying them because I hadn't been sleeping or eating, but I simply didn't have time or energy to worry about what they thought. I had to keep going, working to keep up because I knew that if I didn't, the bakery simply wouldn't be able to open its doors the following day, so I pushed on.

III

THREE DAYS AFTER BEAUCOUP OPENED, THERE WAS A strange lull, a quiet and unusual caesura amid the craziness that preceded it. It was Christmas Eve and I was at the bakery, working. I felt alone. G and I had finally separated just months before, and being apart on Christmas felt strange. We had spent the last eight holidays together, me making a big turkey dinner with two pies and dozens of sides, taking days to prepare. We took particular care in choosing our Christmas trees each year, pulling out the same ornaments and decorations and repeating the same rituals. Each year, I was delighted to see my favorite ornaments, the little feathery birds and real pinecones, and little twinkly lights shining through glassy, coral-colored leaves that made the tree shine in elegant autumn colors.

That Christmas Eve, our first after we split, I invited G to eat with me. He didn't have family in Vancouver, and even if we were not together, I still cared if he spent Christmas alone. But I also missed him and it felt odd not to be together. So he came to the empty bakery at night, while many others were with family celebrating holiday feasts. We sat at a small marble table, ate cheese scones and leftover turkey soup I had frozen from Thanksgiving, and chatted lightheartedly. I was relieved that the most painful parts of our marriage had ended, but I was in pain over the fact it had come to an end at all.

We saw each other, even if just for little visits, each Christmas afterward. Once it was because he asked me for a particular ornament shaped like a bird. Because we had many, I brought him the wrong one, although it was the only one I had found. He seemed disappointed and told me the one we had bought in Bend, Oregon many years ago had special meaning for him. I was touched and confused as to why this one in particular meant so much to him, but didn't ask. I looked again but never found it.

IV

THOUGH I HAD SO MUCH HELP DURING BEAUCOUP'S opening weeks, there was still much more to be done, and the only way for it all to be finished was to work seventy-two hours at a time, with only a few hours of sleep in between. Many nights I simply slept on the concrete floor, not even bothering to put a coat under me, thinking that it would take up a few more seconds of rest I could otherwise have. Often I wore a baking timer on my apron and would forget that it was running. I would see it later that day, only to realize that twenty-four hours had passed and though I had not stopped working, there was still more to do.

This went on for several weeks although, frankly, I'm unsure how. I was simultaneously training my staff, working in the kitchen, serving customers in the café, making the product, and doing the administration, the scheduling, and the ordering—and by no means was I doing it well.

I was irritable and forgetful, leaving timers everywhere, burning trays of cookies and croissants to a shade of black I didn't know existed. Schedules were late and I missed paydays, and some of my team began to feel very undervalued. The customers began to complain because holiday music was still playing in February. I was sorry and exhausted. I wished I had more to give, but really, I didn't.

V

I CROUCHED OVER AND CAUGHT A FAINT SCENT OF SOMETHING extremely familiar. Immediately, I inspected the bottom of my shoes. I had been carrying a box up a ladder to our storage space. Mysterious. I hadn't walked outside in weeks, so how would I have stepped in anything? I sniffed around, investigating, and as the smell followed me around it dawned on me that it was on me.

For weeks, I had barely eaten. There were times I didn't have time to finish chewing or even to swallow, so if an urgent response was needed, I would spit everything out so I could talk. And when I did eat, it was something easy that I could swallow without much chewing at all—more often than not, it was a scone or a cookie.

After weeks of this, my entire body shut down and I no longer had the ability to digest the little food I ate. I smelled myself and realized I had shit my pants and didn't even know it. "How long have I been working like this for?" I asked myself, too tired to laugh, cry, or care. I went to the bathroom to clean myself up, took off my underwear, wrapped it in a plastic bag, and continued to work.

On occasions when I seemed on the brink of collapse, making robotic motions in the kitchen with my eyes completely empty of thought, my staff would push me out of the bakery, threatening to choke me with the string of my apron if I didn't leave for a nap. I distinctly remember one morning I walked through the front door of my nearly empty apartment (which never did feel like a home after G left). I panicked when I saw all the lights on. "Someone must have broken in!" I thought in dread. Then it dawned on me that it was simply daytime, and I had not seen my own home in the daylight for so long, I had forgotten what it looked like.

I laughed at myself and proceeded to bed for a nap. I woke up a few hours later to an alarm, covered in my own excrement again. I had just enough time to shower and leave the mess. Hours or days later, I'm not sure, I came back home ready for sleep, and I was so exhausted I couldn't deal with the mess. So I put the blanket on top and simply slept on it. I really don't remember how long this went on before someone offered to clean my apartment, and found it.

"Um . . . Jackie . . . So I found something strange in your bed," they called me to tell me. They seemed a mixture of surprised, amused, and worried.

"Yeah? What?" I responded, my mind elsewhere.

"Shit."

"Oh yeah. Sorry," I said nonchalantly. I wasn't embarrassed; I was too preoccupied with all the other tasks. So I hung up.

But this is the amazing part: no matter how tired I was or how much work I put in, I don't remember ever feeling unhappy. It was just what needed to be done in order for my dream to have a chance of succeeding. I was willing to do anything, and I felt relieved to see people filing in each day and telling me how much they loved it, or that it reminded them of France. I was pouring everything I had into Beaucoup: all my hopes, my passions, my love, and also the pain of my failed marriage. I desperately wanted to prove that I could be happy, that everything would be beautiful, because it had to be. It was all I had.

VI

IT WAS LATE, I WAS TIRED AND ALONE, ROLLING CROISSANTS
to the sound of the radio. Feeling so exhausted, and with maybe a
touch of self-pity, I crouched on the floor of the kitchen and cried,
hoping that letting it out would make me feel better. But just as
the tears began to fall, I stopped. The longer I cried, the less time
I would have to sleep later, I realized, and it frankly didn't seem
worth it. Everything I desperately wanted was finally happening:
my bakery existed, and there were people coming, and it seemed
silly to cry, so I stopped and went back to rolling croissants.

Years later, my team would reminisce about the early days,
and I realized that I had no recollection of so much of the six
months after we opened. Some memories were probably so hideous that I forgot them out of embarrassment.

There was the three-question rule. In the beginning, my staff
came to me with multitudes of questions, as I was the only person
who knew the answers to "Should I say yes to this special order?"
or "Is this done baking?" The questions became unbearable with
everyone asking the same one more than twice.

In an ideal world, I would have written a guide holding all
the answers and made everyone memorize it, but I didn't know
how to open a bakery. And the questions came, constantly and
repetitively, when I was already doing three things at one time.
So I made a rule: each person was only allowed to ask me three
questions a day. I hoped this would force them to remember,
collaborate, share their answers, and use their precious questions wisely.

One morning, one of my chefs walked into the kitchen when
I was in the middle of baking for the day and planning the next
day in my mind, all the while being utterly sleep-deprived.

"Good morning Jackie! How are you?" she asked cheerfully.

"Good. That was question number one," I said, looking her in the eyes sternly. And then I walked away. My team teased me about it later; it's a vague recollection, like a dream.

VII

MONTHS PASSED AND SEVENTY-TWO HOURS TURNED TO forty-eight, which turned to twenty-four, and I started to get more than a few naps here and there.

As everyone began to learn their roles and become proficient in them, I started to give them more responsibility, until one day I could wildly imagine that the bakery would run for a week without me. So I went to Paris for the first time in years. When I came back, everything was fine, in fact, even more beautiful than I had left it because everyone in the team had come together to make it their own.

VIII

YEARS AFTER THE BAKERY OPENED, MY ROLE HAD CHANGED again. I had realized that my best role was not working day after day in the kitchen, but in directing, fostering, and promoting the business. Naturally, a path led me to focus on marketing, mentoring, and trying to make sure that Beaucoup inspired in everything we did, which was my biggest intention. I began to follow opportunities to write, speak, and judge, and I expanded my vision into The Paris Tours. I also began creating scholarships.

"There was a time I thought I would be tied to the oven," I thought while sitting in a park in Paris one January. "There was a time when I thought I'd never travel again, and a time I thought

I would never see Paris again." I smiled. Life is strange and curious, and I felt extremely grateful for the way it turned out, knowing it could not have been any other way.

"You're not the kitchen type, Jackie," a friend said to me shortly before Beaucoup opened. She saw that this unsettled me. "You won't stay there forever, and it's OK. You're meant to do other things." Sitting on the park bench in Paris, I understood what she meant, though a small part of me was a touch mournful that I never had the chance to learn every one of my customers' names, or their children's birthdays, and that I hadn't been able to give them a cookie or coffee on those days. I always worked for Beaucoup to give the same hope and comfort that food had given me once, even if I am no longer the one at the oven for seventy-two hours at a time.

IX

I RECENTLY WENT BACK TO PROVENCE. IT WAS EARLY summer, and I made a special trip to some of the places I had been before out of a strange kind of nostalgia and a need to heal the painful memories that still remained in me so many years later. I needed to relive the beauty and sorrow I felt there with G, and I knew that being immersed in those places, the details, smells, and tastes, would unearth memories buried deep inside me, ones I was ready to remember. So I visited the markets in L'Isle-sur-la-Sorgue and dined at the hilltop restaurant in Bonnieux, and bought the same fresh cheeses covered in woody herbs to eat on a sunny step.

One afternoon, while exploring Saint-Rémy-de-Provence, I happened into a tiny store, and there, hanging on a twirling rack, were dozens of the same bird ornaments we had bought in Oregon a decade ago. So I bought one for G, and texted him. "I could never find that bird ornament you wanted. Then I was in a small town in Provence and saw one just like it. I'll give it to you next Christmas with some Mexican wedding cookies. How does that sound?"

X

THERE ARE RARE MOMENTS NOWADAYS WHEN I HAPPEN to be at the bakery by myself. It's quiet, just the clunking noise of the espresso machine and a low hum of the refrigerators. I like to sit in the corner. In these moments I experience a mixture of feelings. I'm reminded of those beginning days of Beaucoup, and my body shudders at the memory of everything I put it through. I think of the bakery full of people, and I'm overcome with enormous waves of disbelief and gratitude. I think of all the beautiful pastries my team and I create every single day, and the people who come in and eat and are satisfied. I imagine that maybe someone who felt sad one day came to be fed, and that maybe they left a bit happier. I've been in crowded rooms while people discuss my bakery with emphatic delight, unaware that it is mine, and I feel a rush of pride and gratitude for all the passionate people who have had a hand in creating this dream with me.

I think to myself, it's unreal that I can touch the marble tables I designed, that I am sitting in one of the chairs I spent hours searching for, that it actually exists, this dream.

THE MEASURE OF MY POWERS

{2016}

TO BE HAPPY YOU MUST HAVE TAKEN

the measure of your powers, TASTED THE FRUITS

OF YOUR PASSION, *and* LEARNED YOUR

PLACE *in the* WORLD.

George Santayana

ONE NIGHT, WHILE VISITING PARIS AGAIN—AS I OFTEN do now—I spoke to a dear love over the phone. I was reminded of the past and how painful it was. I cried, and I told him I was terrified of being so sad again, of being swallowed by the pain of depression again.

And he said to me, with so much love in his heart, "Of all the things you've accomplished in your life, the one you should be most proud of is that you have truly learned to love yourself."

My dear love was right. I was no longer the same woman, and there was no reason to be afraid anymore. I had grown, seen, lost, and learned to love, above all myself. It was through seeing the beauty of the world that I began to recognize it in myself, and I learned that the world is beautiful and that I was no different.

So the time had come to let go again, to release my fears so that I could live freely as who I am. And though I will continue to grow and hurt and laugh and cry, I know now that I am also strong, wise, and incredibly brave.

A RECIPE FOR SEEING BEAUTY

1 beautiful rose, sweet smelling

Place the rose near your face. Allow its silky petals to graze your cheek, and close your eyes. Take a breath in, your nose deep in its center so that the blossom surrounds your face and almost hits your eyelashes. Consider its fragrance. Ask yourself, "Does it smell vaguely of anise? Or of pineapples? Or of apricots?"

Afterward, place the blossom in a cup—any cup will do—and set it beside your bed, on the windowsill or a table, beside a book you've been reading, or a journal, or your glasses. And when you wake up the following day, keep your eyes closed and breathe in the lovely scent again before opening your eyes to the morning.

ACKNOWLEDGMENTS

TO ROBERT MCCULLOUGH, who first suggested this memoir: thank you for your graciousness and foresight.

TO BHAVNA CHAUHAN, who deeply understood this book's every intention and, with elegance, challenged me to be more vulnerable, bringing the book to life.

TO JOANN PAI, thank you for telling me what I already knew: that I should just write this book despite being afraid to do so. Your bravery inspires me.

TO JOE CHAN, thank you for reading every chapter back to me as I wrote it, and then patiently listening to me read every word back to you many times over.

TO G's MOM, thank you for sharing with me your love of books and words.

TO G, thank you for all of the years we spent side by side. I wouldn't change a single moment.

TO LIANNE LA HAVAS, though I have never met you, at one time you gave a voice to my mute mourning and my good goodbyes. Thank you.